I0820633

DAY BY DAY WITH THE CATECHISM

". . . May this Catechism be known and shared by everyone, so that the unity in faith . . . may be strengthened and extended to the ends of the earth."

Pope John Paul II, *Laetamur Magnopere*

DAY BY DAY WITH THE CATECHISM

MINUTE MEDITATIONS FOR EVERY DAY CONTAINING AN EXCERPT FROM THE CATECHISM, A REFLECTION, AND A PRAYER

By
Peter A. Giersch

Illustrated

CATHOLIC BOOK PUBLISHING CORP.
New Jersey

CONTENTS

NIHIL OBSTAT: Rev. Msgr. James M. Cafone, M.A., S.T.D.
Censor Librorum

IMPRIMATUR: ✠ Most Rev. John J. Myers, J.C.D., D.D.
Archbishop of Newark

(T-187)

Printed in China 22 HA 2
catholicbookpublishing.com

INTRODUCTION

WHEN I first heard that a revised version of the *Catechism* was to be released in the early 1990s, I expected a multi-volume encyclopedia-like affair. After all, the *Catechism of the Catholic Church* is "a compendium of all Catholic doctrine regarding faith and morals." That sounds rather daunting. Yet, the book itself is surprisingly short—the paperback version is no bigger than an airport novel.

Just being able to hold it in my hand, figure out the organization of it, and flip through the index in the back made it seem manageable to me. So I began to read it on Sunday afternoons when the house was quiet and the experience was almost always a devotional one for me.

The *Catechism* is essentially a reference book, but unlike other reference books, I didn't pick it up to settle a dispute or clarify an issue, and then close it up and place it back on the shelf again. Rather, like poetry or philosophy, I found myself reading two or three lines, then staring out the window for ten minutes with the book open on my lap to the same page while I pondered what I had just read.

And yet, in the Catholic circles I moved in I found very few other people who were reading the *Catechism*, and even heard some people saying that the *Catechism* wasn't meant for the laity to read. That is when I first got the idea for a book like this. When I discovered the "Day by Day" series from Catholic Book Publishing, I knew I had found the right format.

The book is arranged so that the reader can spend a few minutes every day with the official text of the *Catechism*. Selecting these 366 sound bites was probably the most difficult part of the whole project. There were many beautiful passages to choose from, but what is recorded here represents less than one paragraph from every other page.

Nevertheless, these short excerpts from the *Catechism* are rich and pregnant with meaning. Each is followed by a reflection, and a brief prayer rounds out each day.

Here is a traditional method for reading a devotional book like this. Pick it up each day either in the morning or in the evening when things are quiet and you won't be interrupted. First, read the excerpt from the *Catechism* for that day. Read it over several times until a sentence, a phrase, or even just a word, jumps out at you, and spend some time thinking about it.

Next, after you have read the quotation from the *Catechism*, read the reflection, which intends to illuminate the text. You may want to read the text again after reading the reflection. Finally, if you aren't already talking to God about what you've read so far, use the prayer as an aid to raising your mind and heart to God.

It is my hope that this book will whet your appetite to interact with the full text of the *Catechism* yourself. The best place to begin is to make sure you have a copy of it on your shelf.

My special thanks go to Tom Harbecke for his invaluable help keying in the *Catechism* quotations, commenting on the content of the reflections, and proofreading the final version of the text.

Peter A. Giersch
September 30, 2005
Feast of St. Jerome

OD . . . in a plan of sheer goodness freely created man to make him share in his own blessed life. For this reason, at every time and in every place, God draws close to man. —No. 1

JAN. 1

REFLECTION. The first and most amazing truth about life is this: God is seeking us. We so often feel that the Christian life is all about finding God, but in fact, it is about being found *by* God, who draws close to us.

PRAYER. *Father of love, we long to draw close to you. Keep us from running away and hiding like Adam in the garden. Help us to accept your offer to share in the divine life.*

HOSE who with God's help have welcomed Christ's call and freely responded to it are urged on by love of Christ to proclaim the Good News everywhere in the world.` —No. 3

JAN. 2

REFLECTION. When the gospel writers compiled the events of Christ's life, they called their work, *evangelion*, or "good news." These two English words say much about our faith, of course, that it is *good*, but also that it is *news*, it must be shared.

PRAYER. *Father of the Word Incarnate, help us to spread the Word and share the good news of Jesus' life and work by what we say and how we live.*

UITE early on, the name *catechesis* was given to the totality of the Church's efforts to make disciples, to help men believe that Jesus is the Son of God.† —No. 4

JAN. 3

REFLECTION. The good news of the Gospel is set apart from contemporary news in that it is *good*, but more importantly because it builds up and strengthens those who hear it, inviting them into the Body of Christ.

PRAYER. *Jesus, help us to live the dignity that is ours as members of your body. May we always look to you, our head, for guidance and example.*

"

ATECHESIS is an *education in the faith* . . . which includes especially the teaching of Christian doctrine imparted in a systematic way."†† —No. 5

JAN. 4

REFLECTION. While the devout Catholic is always learning about his faith, through prayer, Bible reading, and attendance at Mass, true catechesis demands that there be times of systematic learning about the faith and an intentional commitment to grow in our knowledge of God.

PRAYER. *Father of Creation, you who made the universe in such beauty and order, raise up for us the best teachers, programs, and resources that we may grow in our knowledge and love for you.*

† CT 1, 2.
†† Cf. CT 18.

[THE *Catechism of the Catholic Church*] aims at presenting an organic synthesis of the essential and fundamental contents of Catholic doctrine, as regards both faith and morals. —No. 11

JAN. 5

REFLECTION. The *Catechism* doesn't attempt to be an encyclopedia that passes judgment on every human activity. Rather, the Church speaks to us about faith and morals, knowing that the good life begins with what we believe and how we act.

PRAYER. *Father, so many things are vying for our time and attention. Help us to focus on that which is most important, our relationship with you.*

THE plan of this Catechism . . . [is built] on four pillars: the baptismal profession of faith (the *Creed*), the sacraments of faith, the life of faith (the *Commandments*), and the prayer of the believer (the *Lord's Prayer*). —No. 13

JAN. 6

REFLECTION. These four essential elements of our faith were taught to many of us when we were children, but we cannot let our understanding of these great pillars of the faith remain at an immature level.

PRAYER. *Lord, give us the courage to make full use of all that you have given us to know you to the best of our ability.*

"THE whole concern of doctrine and its teaching must be directed to the love that never ends."† —No. 25

JAN. 7

REFLECTION. As we strive to grow in our lives as Catholic Christians, there is one clear measure by which we can check our progress—that is love. Even if one memorizes the entire *Catechism*, it is of no use if one does not grow in love because of it.

PRAYER. *Sacred Heart of Jesus, make our hearts like your heart so that we may have a deep and sincere love for everyone we meet.*

FAITH is man's response to God, who reveals himself and gives himself to man, at the same time bringing man a superabundant light as he searches for the ultimate meaning of his life. —No. 26

JAN. 8

REFLECTION. Every act of faith, every religious thought, every prayer and act of charity is really a *re*action. God has initiated everything. Any search for ultimate meaning must begin and end with God.

PRAYER. *Lord, open our eyes and flood them with your light so that we may see the many ways in which you reveal yourself to us.*

† *Roman Catechism*, Preface, 10; cf. 1 Cor 13:8.

THE desire for God is written in the human heart, because man is created by God and for God; and God never ceases to draw man to himself. Only in God will he find the truth and happiness he never stops searching for. —No. 27

JAN. 9

REFLECTION. Picture the prodigal son, slowly plodding toward his Father's house, full of hesitation and doubt, not knowing that already his Father has seen him and is running toward him.

PRAYER. *Father, help us to recognize that you offer all the truth and happiness that we are searching for. Help us to find it in you.*

THIS search for God demands of man every effort of intellect, a sound will, [and] "an upright heart." —No. 30

JAN. 10

REFLECTION. Our minds, our hearts, and our wills are the map, the fuel, and the vehicle we use on our journey toward God. "Getting to God" must be the aim of all our thoughts, our emotions, and our desires.

PRAYER. *All-powerful God, cleanse my mind of every worthless evil or distracting thought. Cleanse my heart of every worthless evil or distracting emotion. Cleanse my will of every worthless evil or distracting desire.*

AN is by nature and vocation a religious being. Coming from God, going toward God, man lives a fully human life only if he freely lives by his bond with God. —No. 44

JAN. 11

REFLECTION. There's a Zen-like irony to this: the only way to be fully human during our time on earth is to commit our lives to an unseen God who calls us to a reality beyond what we can know in our present world.

PRAYER. *Jesus, you promised that if we would seek first the kingdom of heaven, everything else would fall into place. Keep the promise you have made to your servants and supply all our needs.*

OD communicates himself to man gradually. He prepares him to welcome by stages the supernatural Revelation that is to culminate in the person and mission of the incarnate Word, Jesus Christ. —No. 53

JAN. 12

REFLECTION. Whether taken over the course of history or in our own brief story, God's relationship with his creatures grows and deepens over time, in a million small moments. We draw near or create distance with every choice we make.

PRAYER. *Lord of creation, by your all-wise plan, everything grows. Help us to grow in our knowledge of you through the constant purification of our mind, heart, and will.*

FTER the unity of the human race was shattered by sin God at once sought to save humanity part by part. —No. 56

JAN. 13

REFLECTION. As much as we need light, we do know the experience of "too bright." Just as we go from darkness to light gradually, so God brought the human race from sin to salvation "part by part," over time, as the dawn gently and beautifully brings the day to chase away the night.

PRAYER. *Lord, make this day one more step toward you, our ultimate goal.*

HRIST, the Son of God made man, is the Father's one, perfect, and unsurpassable Word. In him he has said everything; there will be no other word than this one. —No. 65

JAN. 14

REFLECTION. The perfect way in which Christ articulated and fulfilled God's message of love strains our human vocabulary. St. Paul struggled to express it with phrases like, "the fullness of him who fills all in all."†

PRAYER. *Father, do not let us chase after false teachers, or seek signs in nature and prophecies in the occult; make us open our hearts and minds to Jesus Christ, your Word.*

† Eph 1:23.

EVEN if Revelation is already complete, it has not been made completely explicit; it remains for Christian faith gradually to grasp its full significance over the course of the centuries. —No. 66

JAN. 15

REFLECTION. The beauty of Christian life is that there is always more to it: more truth to be grasped, more richness to be experienced, more beauty to be enjoyed, and more love to give and receive.

PRAYER. *Lord, all that my faith is today is but a little compared to what it can be. Inspire me to set out into the deep!*

THE Church has always venerated the Scriptures as she venerates the Lord's Body. She never ceases to present to the faithful the bread of life, taken from the one table of God's Word and Christ's Body.† —No. 103

JAN. 16

REFLECTION. The Mass is primarily an experience of Christ. In the readings we encounter Christ "the Word," and in the Eucharist we are fed by Jesus, "the Bread of Life."

PRAYER. *Jesus, you reveal your beauty and love in the Holy Sacrifice of the Mass. May we come to church ready to meet you in word and in the flesh.*

† Cf. DV 21.

"IN the sacred books, the Father who is in heaven comes lovingly to meet his children, and talks with them."† —No. 104

JAN. 17

REFLECTION. It has often been said that when we pray we speak to God, and when we read the Bible he speaks to us. In our relationship with God, we need to make sure we're not doing all the talking.

PRAYER. *Lord, inspire us and give us the strength to read the Bible regularly that it may bear fruit in a well-ordered life of wisdom.*

THE Old Testament is an indispensable part of Sacred Scripture. Its books are divinely inspired and retain a permanent value,†† for the Old Covenant has never been revoked. —No. 121

JAN. 18

REFLECTION. God spent a long time preparing the world for his Son, and the whole fascinating process is chronicled in the Old Testament, an important part of the greatest story ever told.

PRAYER. *Father of Abraham, Isaac, and Jacob, reveal yourself to us through the history, the prophets, and the wisdom of the Hebrew Scriptures.*

† DV 21.
†† Cf. DV 14.

THE *Gospels* are the heart of all the Scriptures "because they are our principal source for the life and teaching of the Incarnate Word, our Savior."†

—No. 125

JAN. 19

REFLECTION. St. Jerome says, "Ignorance of Scripture is ignorance of Christ." This is especially true where the four Gospels are concerned. Every effort to know Christ better must include a deep familiarity with Matthew, Mark, Luke, and John.

PRAYER. *Father of our Lord Jesus Christ, unfold for your people the mystery of your Word made flesh through the sacred writings of the Evangelists.*

THE Church "forcefully and specifically exhorts all the Christian faithful . . . to learn 'the surpassing knowledge of Jesus Christ,' by frequent reading of the divine Scriptures."†† —No. 133

JAN. 20

REFLECTION. So often we know the solution, but lack the willpower. The value of a healthy diet and exercise are never in question, but it is a challenge to pursue them. So it is with daily Bible reading. There is no question it will improve your life. It is simply a matter of choosing to do it.

PRAYER. *Lord, we are weak creatures of the flesh; strengthen our will.*

† DV 18.
†† DV 25; cf. Phil 3:8.

Y *faith* man completely submits his intellect and his will to God.† With his whole being, man gives his assent to the revealer. —No. 143

JAN. 21

REFLECTION. It seems like such a difficult choice to turn our whole lives over to God, but to think that a creature can have anything of value apart from the Creator is utter self-delusion.

PRAYER. *Father, you are constantly pouring yourself out for us, through your Son by the working of the Holy Spirit. Help us to respond to your generosity by our faith in you.*

HE Virgin Mary most perfectly embodies the obedience of faith. By faith, Mary welcomes the tidings and promise brought by the angel Gabriel, believing that "with God nothing will be impossible."†† —No. 148

JAN. 22

REFLECTION. The first chapter of Luke captures the beginning of God's plan of salvation in two of the most beautiful stories in Scripture—the Annunciation and the Visitation. Though just a little girl, Mary's faith and obedience are as great as any other hero of the Bible.

PRAYER. *Lord, increase our faith! May the prayers of the Virgin Mary support our efforts to believe in you.*

† Cf. DV 5.

†† Lk 1:37-38; cf. Gen 18:14.

CHRISTIAN faith differs from our faith in any human person. It is right and just to entrust oneself wholly to God and to believe absolutely what he says. —No. 150

JAN. 23

REFLECTION. We live in an age of skepticism, when everything is held under suspicion, and even engaged couples make exit strategies. Our faith in God must not be influenced by the spirit of our age. With God there is no risk of betrayal.

PRAYER. *Jesus, you are the Truth that sets us free from sin and error. May we commit ourselves to you without reservation.*

ONE cannot believe in Jesus Christ without sharing in his Spirit. It is the Holy Spirit who reveals to men who Jesus is. —No. 152

JAN. 24

REFLECTION. As natural as it should be for a creature to trust her Creator, we need help to do this consistently and well. God knows this and sends his Spirit to help us enter into the divine life of the Trinity.

PRAYER. *Lord, send out your Spirit to inspire true faith in you. May we come to know you with all our strength of mind and heart and will.*

AITH makes us taste in advance the light of the beatific vision, the goal of our journey here below. —No. 163

JAN. 25

REFLECTION. Unlike hope, which is focused on the future, faith has the power to bring our desires into being in the present that we may experience them now, if only in a partial way. As the Bible says, "faith is the assurance of things hoped for."†

PRAYER. *Lord, may our faith in your promise of eternal happiness fill us with an unshakable joy.*

AITH is a personal act. . . . But faith is not an isolated act. No one can believe alone, just as no one can live alone. —No. 166

JAN. 26

REFLECTION. The family, community, and political society are all structures that teach us how to live in this world. In the same way, our family, our parish, and the universal Church are all channels whereby the faith is planted in us, nurtures, and grows.

PRAYER. *Jesus, you learned the ways of faith from the Virgin Mary and St. Joseph. May we benefit from their prayers and live by their example.*

† Heb 11:1.

ALVATION comes from God alone; but because we receive the light of faith through the Church, she is our mother. —No. 169

JAN. 27

REFLECTION. The natural curiosity many people show in their genealogy is shared by the Church, which keeps diligent records of the passing on of the faith through the preservation of ancient Christian writings, through apostolic succession of bishops, and through sacramental records of the faithful.

PRAYER. *Father, we thank you for the family of believers you have brought together under the protection of your Church. Keep us safe in the Church until death.*

O say the [Creed] with faith is to enter into communion with God, Father, Son, and Holy Spirit, and also with the whole Church which transmits the faith to us and in whose midst we believe. —No. 197

JAN. 28

REFLECTION. Prayer, even at its most personal and private, is always a social act. As members of the Body of Christ, every prayer is shared, and each member participates in the prayer of the whole Church.

PRAYER. *Father, draw us into a deeper union with you through the universal faith and unity of your people, the Church.*

THE beginning of sin and of man's fall was due to a lie of the tempter who induced doubt of God's word, kindness, and faithfulness. —No. 215

JAN. 29

REFLECTION. Satan does not own any guns or bombs. He does not sell drugs or solicit prostitutes. His only weapon is to lie. All he can do is convince us to believe lies about God, ourselves, and our future, and all the evil he intends will follow.

PRAYER. *Jesus, inspire in us a great love for the truth, that we may know the freedom it brings and recognize the evil of lies and deception.*

IN THE course of its history, Israel was able to discover that God had only one reason to reveal himself to them, a single motive for choosing them from among all peoples as his special possession: his sheer gratuitous love.† —No. 218

JAN. 30

REFLECTION. Love is what caused the creation of the universe. This love flows from God and is directed at all of his creation, but primarily at us, creatures made in his image.

PRAYER. *Father, pour your love into our hearts that the Holy Spirit may dwell with us and produce in us love, joy, and peace.*

† Cf. Deut 4:37; 7:8; 10:15.

ELIEVING in God, the only One, and loving him with all our being has enormous consequences for our whole life. —No. 222

JAN. 31

REFLECTION. When we truly start to believe what we profess, everything changes. We are humbled by the majesty of God, dignified by his glory shining in us and in others, and we rejoice in the beauty of his creation. This life of humility, dignity, and joy is a sign of a true believer.

PRAYER. *Lord, may this faith we profess make such a difference in our lives that all we do may lead to your glory and our salvation.*

HE mystery of the Most Holy Trinity is the central mystery of Christian faith and life. It is the mystery of God in himself. It is therefore the source of all the other mysteries of faith, the light that enlightens them. —No. 234

FEB. 1

REFLECTION. The issue of identity is at the center of all the questions of our life. "Who am I?" and "Who are you?" are lifelong meditations that flow from, and are enriched by, the doctrine of the Trinity.

PRAYER. *Father, faced with the mystery of our identity we find comfort in the sure knowledge that we are your children.*

THE whole Christian life is a communion with each of the divine persons, without in any way separating them. —No. 259

FEB. 2

REFLECTION. Although there is only one God who reaches out to us in love, at different times in our life we might relate to different aspects of God: the power and majesty of the Creator, the intimacy of Christ our brother, or the charismatic fire of the Holy Spirit.

PRAYER. *God, I commit my life to you in the name of the Father, and of the Son, and of the Holy Spirit. Amen.*

THE ultimate end of the whole divine economy is the entry of God's creatures into the perfect unity of the Blessed Trinity.† —No. 260

FEB. 3

REFLECTION. The human being is an awesome creature whose full dignity is rarely understood. Yet, our destiny in God is even greater than all that we are now: it is no less than true participation in the divine life of the Trinity.

PRAYER. *Father, you sent your Son to become like us so that we could become like you. By the work of the Holy Spirit, help us to grow in the likeness of Christ your Son.*

† Cf. Jn 17:21-23.

OF ALL the divine attributes, only God's omnipotence is named in the Creed: to confess this power has great bearing on our lives. —No. 268

FEB. 4

REFLECTION. To believe in a God who is all powerful and can do whatever he wills is to admit our own insignificance. To call this omnipotent God "Father" is to claim an extraordinary dignity.

PRAYER. *God our Father, keep us ever mindful of your power at work in the world, and of your love at work in our lives.*

GOD can sometimes seem to be absent and incapable of stopping evil. But in the most mysterious way God the Father has revealed his almighty power in the voluntary humiliation and Resurrection of his Son, by which he conquered evil. —No. 272

FEB. 5

REFLECTION. The mysterious way in which God uses strength and weakness to bring about good is a counter-cultural example for us in a world where might makes right.

PRAYER. *Father, your grace is all we need. Let your power shine most perfectly in our weakness that we may be witnesses to your kind of might.*

ATECHESIS on creation is of major importance. It concerns the very foundations of human and Christian life. —No. 282

FEB. 6

REFLECTION. Arguments over the theory of evolution can easily distract us from the importance of reflecting on God as Creator. Putting aside all the theories and meditating on the simple statement "nothing comes from nothing" is one way to begin our catechesis on creation.

PRAYER. *Creator God, let us learn from the world around us of your greatness and love. May all that you have made point us back to you.*

REATION . . . did not spring forth complete from the hands of the Creator. The universe was created "in a state of journeying" (*in statu viae*) toward an ultimate perfection yet to be attained, to which God has destined it. —No. 302

FEB. 7

REFLECTION. Everything is in the process of becoming something else. As obvious as this seems, it is of tremendous importance, because it is this unfinished state of the universe that allows for concepts like hope, anticipation, optimism, and potential.

PRAYER. *Father, you promise us a future full of hope. Draw us to that life of eternal unity with you, our ultimate goal.*

OD is the sovereign master of his plan. But to carry it out, he also makes use of his creatures' cooperation. —No. 306

FEB. 8

REFLECTION. True cooperation creates mysteriously. It is hard to tell where the work of one ends and another begins. This is how the world looks to the Christian. It seems that all is God, and yet, each of our decisions has such undeniable impact.

PRAYER. *Father, be patient with us. As we strive to do what would please you, support our efforts and guide us in the path of your commands, for there we find joy.*

RAWN from nothingness by God's power, wisdom, and goodness, [the creature] can do nothing if it is cut off from its origin, for "without a Creator the creature vanishes."† —No. 308

FEB. 9

REFLECTION. Look into the faces of the people you will interact with today and contemplate the fact that each of these people was "drawn out of nothingness" by God to be here, looking into your face. Reflect on God's desire to create the other person.

PRAYER. *Lord, you love everything you have created. Let all the people you willed to be give you praise by the witness of their lives.*

† GS 36:3.

HY does evil exist? . . . Only Christian faith as a whole constitutes the answer to this question. . . . ***There is not a single aspect of the Christian message that is not in part an answer to the question of evil.*** —No. 309

FEB. 10

REFLECTION. Many ask, "How can there be a God with so much evil in the world?" Christianity asks a different question: "If there is no God, how does one explain virtue, love, and all the good they have inspired?"

PRAYER. *Father, we are your people. Let our lives manifest your presence and weaken the power of evil.*

N TIME we can discover that God in his almighty providence can bring a good from the consequences of an evil. . . . But for all that, evil never becomes a good. —No. 312

FEB. 11

REFLECTION. Even though we know that God can bring good out of the most difficult circumstances of our lives, we must never trivialize our trials or those of others. The scourge of evil was not God's original intention for the universe.

PRAYER. *Jesus, you sweat blood meditating on the evil of the world; help us to understand the true consequences of our actions.*

NGELS have been present since creation and throughout the history of salvation, announcing this salvation from afar or near and serving the accomplishment of the divine plan.

—No. 332

FEB. 12

REFLECTION. God could have saved the world with a word, but he chose mediators to accomplish the work. First and foremost he sent his Son Jesus Christ; next, he uses the prayers of Mary and all the Saints. Nearest to us are his Angels who assist us on our way to him.

PRAYER. *Holy Angels, come to our aid! Guardian Angel, protect me and lead me to Christ.*

OD wills *the interdependence of creatures*. . . . Creatures exist only in dependence on each other, to complete each other, in the service of each other. **—No. 340**

FEB. 13

REFLECTION. All this talk of consenting adults, rights of privacy, and civil liberties is counterproductive when it presents the individual as an isolated, self-contained unit, free to act without reference to the rest of society. Such a view of the human person is false.

PRAYER. *Christ, teach us to need our neighbors, to seek and give help, that we might come to know the blessings of unity.*

AN is the summit **of the Creator's work, as the inspired account expresses by clearly distinguishing the creation of man from that of the other creatures.† —No. 343**

FEB. 14

REFLECTION. We often hear it said of humans that "we are just another animal," though everything from art to airplanes seems to prove otherwise. As children of God we must cherish our privileged status and gravely own up to the responsibility that goes with it.

PRAYER. *Father in heaven, as your children, may we always be mindful of the dignity that is ours.*

EING in the image of God, the human individual possesses the dignity of a person, who is not just something, but someone. —No. 357

FEB. 15

REFLECTION. The only beings in the known universe who share the title of "person" are humans, angels, and the three divine persons of the Holy Trinity, Father, Son, and Holy Spirit. We are in good company.

PRAYER. *Triune God, Father, Son, and Holy Spirit, help us to fully live our personhood, which we share with you.*

† Cf. Gen 1:26.

THE human person, created in the image of God, is a being at once corporeal and spiritual. —No. 362

FEB. 16

REFLECTION. To be fully human, one needs to be fully in touch with both the physical and the spiritual realities of our lives. We need to feed both body and spirit, never neglecting one or the other.

PRAYER. *God of spirit and of matter, help us to serve you with our whole beings, as truly integrated persons.*

THE first man was not only created good, but was also established in friendship with his Creator and in harmony with himself and with the creation around him, in a state that would be surpassed only by the glory of the new creation in Christ. —No. 374

FEB. 17

REFLECTION. There are three relationships mentioned here: man with God, with self, and with others. In paradise, all three were in perfect harmony. Our Christian life calls us to restore that harmony.

PRAYER. *Father, help us to live a life of piety, honesty, and justice, that we may know true peace.*

THE "mastery" over the world that God offered man from the beginning was realized above all within man himself: *mastery of self.* —No. 377

FEB. 18

REFLECTION. The interior life—the place where the true self resides—is where we face our greatest challenges, our deepest fears, and our most joyous triumphs. All other types of success begin with self-control, self-knowledge, and self-love.

PRAYER. *Lord, you search me and you know me. Open my eyes that I may know the real me that you see.*

SIN is present in human history; any attempt to ignore it or to give this dark reality other names would be futile. —No. 386

FEB. 19

REFLECTION. It is not always easy to judge whether an act is good or evil, but best to err on the side of caution. It is a human tendency to deny the presence of sin in our lives, and doing so only increases its hold over us.

PRAYER. *Lord, open our eyes to see the truth about ourselves and help us to do what is right and pleasing to you always.*

EHIND the disobedient choice of our first parents lurks a seductive voice, opposed to God, which makes them fall into death out of envy.† —No. 391

FEB. 20

REFLECTION. The devil offers us so much, but in fact, we already possess the very thing he jealously covets but cannot have—union with God. Temptation may feel like a chance to trade misery for pleasure, but it is really the opposite.

PRAYER. *Father, never let us be fooled by the empty promises of the devil. Help us to hold fast to your Word, Jesus Christ.*

APTISM . . . erases original sin and turns man back toward God, but the consequences for nature, weakened and inclined to evil, persist in man and summon him to spiritual battle. —No. 405

FEB. 21

REFLECTION. People either see the devil in everything or deny him altogether. Both of these extremes are dangerous. The truth is in the middle. God is greater than the devil and limits his power, but the pernicious influence of our adversary is undeniable.

PRAYER. *St. Michael, defend us in battle against the wickedness and snares of the devil.*

† Cf. Gen 3:1-5; Wis 2:24.

THE victory that Christ won over sin has given us greater blessings than those which sin had taken from us: "where sin increased, grace abounded all the more."† —No. 420

FEB. 22

REFLECTION. Christians often proclaim that God brings good out of evil, but it might be more accurate to say that God brings "better" out of evil.

PRAYER. *Father, in your mighty plan you have thought of everything, making all things tend toward our benefit. Let this knowledge of your love for us increase our faith in you.*

FROM this loving knowledge of Christ springs the desire to proclaim him, to "evangelize," and to lead others to the "yes" of faith in Jesus Christ. But at the same time the need to know this faith better makes itself felt. —No. 429

FEB. 23

REFLECTION. Telling others about Christ is a great blessing, but it is also a tremendous responsibility. When sharing our faith, we must all distinguish between our own conclusions drawn in isolation and true Christian doctrine.

PRAYER. *Father of the Word Incarnate, make us able and effective evangelizers that all may come to know you.*

† Rom 5:20.

HE name of Jesus is at the heart of Christian prayer. —No. 435

FEB. 24

REFLECTION. Jesus told us to pray in his name, and so we end our prayers saying, "through Christ our Lord." We should be equally mindful that other prayers, such as the Jesus Prayer, the Hail Mary, and the Gloria also find their center of gravity in the sacred name. It is a name that should always be on our minds, on our lips, and in our hearts.

PRAYER. *Jesus Christ, Son of God, have mercy on me, a sinner.*

O CONFESS or invoke Jesus as Lord is to believe in his divinity. "No one can say 'Jesus is Lord' except by the Holy Spirit."† —No. 455

FEB. 25

REFLECTION. There are several facts that are at the heart of our faith. We should return to these touchstones again and again in our lives, grasping them more firmly year by year. "Jesus is God" is one such fact.

PRAYER. *Jesus, help us to grasp the reality of your divinity that the ramifications of that belief may touch our whole lives*

† 1 Cor 12:3.

HE Word became flesh for us *in order to save us by reconciling us with God.* —No. 457

FEB. 26

REFLECTION. Something in us shrinks from God. We are children of an omniscient parent with very high standards, and it is not surprising that we sometimes like to keep our distance. Yet, Christ has made full union with God possible by satisfying his Father's requirements on our behalf.

PRAYER. *Father, you accepted the offering of your Son who died for our sins. May nothing else prevent our complete union with you.*

HE Word became flesh *so that thus we might know God's love.* —No. 458

FEB. 27

REFLECTION. The greatest thinkers and philosophers of the ancient world were only able to go as far as ethics and a sort of utilitarian charity. It took Christianity to articulate love as the center of the human experience.

PRAYER. *Father, with so many signs of your love all around us, may we imitate you in manifesting our love day by day.*

THE Word became flesh to make us *"partakers of the divine nature."*† —No. 460

FEB. 28

REFLECTION. At the center of the New Age Movement is the proclamation that "I am God, and you are too." Like all heresies, it asks the right question, but gets the wrong answer. Can humans be divine? Yes, but only by participation in the divinity of Christ.

PRAYER. *Jesus, you have glorified human nature by your incarnation. Make us one with you in truth.*

JESUS knew and loved us each and all during his life, his agony, and his Passion and gave himself up for each one of us: "The Son of God . . . loved me and gave himself for me."†† —No. 478

FEB. 29

REFLECTION. Despite the many corporate ways in which Christians relate to Christ, as his Body, as his Church, and as his Bride, there is, notwithstanding these realities, an intensely personal and uniquely individual element of our relationship with Jesus.

PRAYER. *Jesus, may I always be mindful that you have chosen to call me friend.*†††

† 2 Pet 1:4.
†† Gal 2:20.
††† Cf. Jn 15:15.

HAT the Catholic faith believes about Mary is based on what it believes about Christ, and what it teaches about Mary illumines in turn its faith in Christ. —No. 487

MAR. 1

REFLECTION. The more firmly we grasp the truth and reality of Jesus' divinity, the more we stand in awe at the dignity and the glory that God has bestowed on Mary by her unique role in the Incarnation.

PRAYER. *Jesus, help us to honor your Mother for the gift you gave her. May our love for you inspire us to honor her ever more.*

GAINST all human expectation God chooses those who were considered powerless and weak to show forth his faithfulness to his promises. —No. 489

MAR. 2

REFLECTION. God chooses whom he wills, but rarely whom we would expect, to carry out his purposes. So it is with Mary. The most highly favored and blessed creature in all of human history was young, a minority, and a woman.

PRAYER. *Father, let us see the dignity in everyone you have made. May Mary's prayers help us to love others as you love them.*

FROM the first formulations of her faith, the Church has confessed that Jesus was conceived solely by the power of the Holy Spirit in the womb of the Virgin Mary. —No. 496

MAR. 3

REFLECTION. The reality of the Virgin Birth is one of those foundational truths of the faith that we should meditate on often and firmly grasp. Jesus' divinity, a point on which our faith so heavily depends, is untenable without the Virgin Birth.

PRAYER. *Father, I do believe in Jesus Christ who was conceived by the Holy Spirit and born of the Virgin Mary. Help me to believe it more firmly.*

MARY'S virginity manifests God's absolute initiative in the Incarnation. Jesus has only God as Father. —No. 503

MAR. 4

REFLECTION. When we speak of the Virgin Birth it is easy to forget that Mary did not bring Jesus into the world alone. At God's initiative, and with her consent, Mary was inseminated by the Holy Spirit. The Church rightly gives her the title, "Spouse of the Holy Spirit."

PRAYER. *Mary, your intimacy with the Trinity was unique among all God's creatures. Pray for us that we may draw closer daily to the Father, the Son, and the Holy Spirit.*

ARY is truly "Mother of God" since she is the mother of the eternal Son of God made man, who is God himself. —No. 509

MAR. 5

REFLECTION. Of all of those who experienced Jesus in the flesh, no one was closer to him than Mary, biologically and emotionally. Of all the relationships in the Bible, the intimacy between Jesus and Mary holds a special place and is a model of human intimacy.

PRAYER. *Jesus, inspire us to love your mother as you loved her. May we always know the blessings of Mary's patronage and intercession.*

HRIST'S whole earthly life—his words and deeds, his silences and sufferings, indeed his manner of being and speaking—is ***Revelation*** of the Father. —No. 516

MAR. 6

REFLECTION. God's revelation of himself, stretched out across all of human history, taking many and varied forms, reaches its greatest intensity in the Incarnation. In Jesus, the incarnate Word, the Father speaks most simply and most powerfully of who he is.

PRAYER. *Jesus, you are the revelation of the Father's love for us. Help us to open wide our hearts and minds to receive all that you long to teach us.*

HRIST enables us *to live in him* all that he himself lived, and *he lives it in us.* —No. 521

MAR. 7

REFLECTION. The imitation of Christ is the goal of every Christian. But we are meant to be more than just actors, mimicking Christ. We are to be channels, animated by Christ himself, as he lives his life in us. His triumphs, sufferings, his glory and all the graces he possessed, he shares with us when we die to self and allow him to live in us.

PRAYER. *Thank you for dying for me, dear Jesus. May I live for you. May you live in me.*

URING the greater part of his life Jesus shared the condition of the vast majority of human beings: a daily life spent without evident greatness, a life of manual labor. —No. 531

MAR. 8

REFLECTION. The ancient Greeks spoke of an "everyman" who represented humanity in all of its diversity. Jesus fulfilled this character perfectly in his life on earth, identifying with all people—but especially the poor and the weak, dignifying their state by his association with them.

PRAYER. *Jesus, you know what it is like to be me. Help me to live my life as you would do.*

ARY "kept all these things in her heart" during the years Jesus remained hidden in the silence of an ordinary life. —No. 534

MAR. 9

REFLECTION. Mary is a model for all Christians. Just as she spent her life in loving meditation on her son Jesus,† so we should contemplate Christ and treasure the mysteries of his life in our hearts. The Rosary is an excellent aid to help us do so.

PRAYER. *Father, bring us to a greater appreciation for the gift of the Rosary that we may use it to meditate more deeply on the life of Christ.*

Y the solemn forty days of *Lent* the Church unites herself each year to the mystery of Jesus in the desert. —No. 540

MAR. 10

REFLECTION. Jesus' retreat into the desert teaches us how to live the Christ-life in many ways. Most importantly, we see the value of solitude, silence, and self-denial in the search for God. Lent is a yearly opportunity to experience again the power of these practices.

PRAYER. *Jesus, may we have the strength, as you did, to deny our human desires so that we may draw closer to God and embrace his will for us.*

† Cf. Lk 2:51.

O those who turn to [Jesus] in faith, he grants what they ask.† —No. 548

MAR. 11

REFLECTION. Jesus promised to answer the prayers of his followers, and during his life, he did so without hesitation time and time again. Despite occasional disappointments with prayers that go (apparently) unanswered, we must believe that God is faithful and never stop asking, seeking, and knocking in prayer and petition.

PRAYER. *Lord, hear and answer the prayers of your people as we turn to you in faith, with confidence in the love you have for us.*

HE Paschal mystery of Christ's cross and Resurrection stands at the center of the Good News that the apostles, and the Church following them, are to proclaim to the world. —No. 571

MAR. 12

REFLECTION. Bible scholars often say that the gospels are "written backwards." For all of their diversity, Matthew, Mark, Luke, and John show an amazing agreement on the Passion, death, and Resurrection of Christ, attesting to what is most important about the story of Jesus.

PRAYER. *Father, help us enter more deeply into the Paschal mystery of your Son so that we may witness to it more effectively in our lives.*

† Cf. Mk 5:25-34; 10:52; etc.

JESUS' violent death was not the result of chance in an unfortunate coincidence of circumstances, but is part of the mystery of God's plan. —No. 599

MAR. 13

REFLECTION. There is an old cultural idiom that says, "The Lord moves in mysterious ways his wonders to perform." By choosing to accomplish our salvation through the violent death of his only Son we come face to face with a God who is mystery.

PRAYER. *Father, help us to understand the value of suffering and to embrace the role that it plays in your loving plan of redemption.*

TO God, all moments of time are present in their immediacy. When therefore he establishes his eternal plan of "predestination," he includes in it each person's free response to his grace.† —No. 600

MAR. 14

REFLECTION. God has so much respect for us that first he lets us make our own choice in response to his activity, then works out his loving plan, never allowing our mistakes and sins to thwart his great design.

PRAYER. *Father, give us wisdom to know your will and strength to carry it out, for in your will is our peace.*

† Acts 4:27-28; cf. Ps 2:1-2.

FROM the first moment of his Incarnation the Son embraces the Father's plan of divine salvation in his redemptive mission: "My food is to do the will of him who sent me, and to accomplish his work."†

—No. 606

MAR. 15

REFLECTION. In the Gospel portrait of Jesus, we see a man on a mission. From the moment of his baptism to his death on the cross Jesus remains focused on fulfilling God's plan for him.

PRAYER. *Lord, help us to overcome all that distracts us so that we may focus on and never waver from our goal to serve you.*

BY embracing in his human heart the Father's love for men, Jesus, "loved them to the end." For "greater love has no man than this, that a man lay down his life for his friends."†† —No. 609

MAR. 16

REFLECTION. Jesus loved us—and still loves us—with a human heart. This is why the Church supports the devotion to the Sacred Heart of Jesus.

PRAYER. *Sacred Heart of Jesus, I believe in your love for me. May I ever love you more and more. Sacred Heart of Jesus, I trust in you.*

† Jn 4:34.
†† Jn 13:1; 15:13.

ECAUSE in his incarnate divine person [Jesus] has in some way united himself to every man, "the possibility of being made partners, in a way known to God, in the paschal mystery" is offered to all men.† **—No. 618**

MAR. 17

REFLECTION. The Catholic Church is sometimes accused of being exclusive, but when it comes to salvation, the Church takes a very liberal view of God's love, seeing the possibility of salvation for all humankind.

PRAYER. *Jesus, lead all souls to heaven, especially those in most need of your mercy.*

N his plan of salvation, God ordained that his Son should not only "die for our sins"†† but should also "taste death," experience the condition of death, the separation of his soul from his body. **— No . 624**

MAR. 18

REFLECTION. We say Christ was like us in everything but sin, and that includes death. Jesus really died. He knows the human experience better than we do. He has faced our biggest fear.

PRAYER. *Jesus, may my faith in you help me to come to terms with my own death.*

† GS 22 § 5; cf. § 2.

†† 1 Cor 15:3.

MAR. 19

JESUS, like all men, experienced death and in his soul joined the others in the realm of the dead. But he descended there as Savior, proclaiming the Good News to the spirits imprisoned there.†

—No. 632

REFLECTION. Without destroying hell, or putting an end to damnation, Jesus gave those who had gone before him a chance to hear the Good News and live. No one is excluded from the redemptive work of Christ.

PRAYER. *Father, your arm is long enough to save anyone who turns to you in truth. Draw all men and women to yourself.*

MAR. 20

THE Resurrection of Jesus is the crowning truth of our faith in Christ, a faith believed and lived as the central truth by the first Christian community; handed on as fundamental by Tradition; established by the documents of the New Testament; and preached as an essential part of the Paschal mystery along with the cross.

—No. 638

REFLECTION. Of all the basic beliefs that a Christian ought to meditate on often, the truth of Jesus' actual resurrection holds a special place.

PRAYER. *I believe that on the third day, Jesus rose from the dead in fulfillment of the Scriptures.*

† Cf. 1 Pet 3:18-19.

THE mystery of Christ's resurrection is a real event, with manifestations that were historically verified, as the New Testament bears witness. —No. 639

MAR. 21

REFLECTION. A real live human being was killed and then rose from the dead. This is not a myth or symbol. Jesus didn't return as a ghost, or merely live on as an inspirational memory. He really rose from the dead. The more honestly we wrestle with that, the more firmly we will believe it.

PRAYER. *Jesus, help me to really know you and to experience the power of your resurrection.*

BY means of touch and the sharing of a meal, the risen Jesus establishes direct contact with his disciples. . . . Yet at the same time this authentic, real body possesses the new properties of a glorious body: not limited by space and time but able to be present how and when he wills.

—No. 645

MAR. 22

REFLECTION. The resurrected Jesus, as he is presented in the Gospels, defies human definition. This is not a ghost, not a resuscitated human, and not an angel, not a dream or an apparition.

PRAYER. *Resurrected Christ, we acknowledge your presence among us. Remain with us always.*

N his risen body [Jesus] passes from the state of death to another life beyond time and space. . . . He shares the divine life in his glorious state, so that St. Paul can say that Christ is "the man of heaven."†

—No. 646

MAR. 23

REFLECTION. There is no question that the disciples were deeply moved by their encounter with the resurrected Christ—and it is no wonder. Imagine being in that presence.

PRAYER. *Risen Christ, may we recognize you in the reading of the Word and the breaking of the Bread.*

ll truths, even those most inaccessible to human reason, find their justification if Christ by his Resurrection has given the definitive proof of his divine authority, which he had promised.

—No. 651

MAR. 24

REFLECTION. By his resurrection from the dead, Christ "earned our trust" so to speak, so that we may embrace even the most difficult of his teachings. It makes no sense to believe the Resurrection but question his power to work miracles, the Eucharist, or hard teachings like "love your enemies."

PRAYER. *Lord, let the truth of your Resurrection take root in our hearts.*

† Cf. 1 Cor 15:35-50.

JESUS Christ, the head of the Church, precedes us into the Father's glorious kingdom so that we, the members of his Body, may live in the hope of one day being with him for ever. —No. 666

MAR. 25

REFLECTION. The Ascension—not the Resurrection—is the real source of our hope. If Jesus' Resurrection only meant living forever on earth, that would not be good news! The Ascension points us to our ultimate destiny beyond this earth.

PRAYER. *Jesus, help us to lift our eyes beyond the borders of this earthly life to our eternal destiny with you.*

JESUS Christ, having entered the sanctuary of heaven once and for all, intercedes constantly for us as the mediator who assures us of the permanent outpouring of the Holy Spirit. —No. 667

MAR. 26

REFLECTION. God uses intermediaries to draw us to himself. Mary and the saints, the angels, the Church, all God's creatures and creation can help bring us closer to God. But the greatest and foremost mediator between God and humanity is his own Son, Jesus Christ.

PRAYER. *Father, may all things draw us closer to you by the working of the Holy Spirit through your Son, Jesus Christ.*

HRIST'S Ascension into heaven signifies his participation, in his humanity, in God's power and authority. Jesus Christ is Lord: he possesses all power in heaven and on earth. —No. 668

MAR. 27

REFLECTION. The Incarnation was not merely an earthly experience. Jesus ascended bodily to heaven where he reigns as true God—and true man—in his glorified body. In Jesus there is a human body that is dignified and glorified.

PRAYER. *Jesus, as man you shared our experience and as God you dignified it.*

S Lord, Christ is also head of the Church, which is his Body.† Taken up to heaven and glorified after he had thus fully accomplished his mission, Christ dwells on earth in his Church. —No. 669

MAR. 28

REFLECTION. Jesus' Incarnation—his physical presence on earth—did not end with the Ascension. In the Church, and especially in the Sacraments, each of us in our own time and in our own way can have a physical encounter with the Incarnate Word.

PRAYER. *Christ, may we who are your Body and your Church always remain close to you, our head.*

† Cf. Eph 1:22.

INCE the Ascension God's plan has entered into its fulfillment. We are already at "the last hour."† —No. 670

MAR. 29

REFLECTION. There is a great deal of speculation about whether or not we are living in "the end times," but, in fact, the Church still proclaims what the first followers of Jesus knew, that the "end of the age" began with the Ascension of Christ and will continue until his return.

PRAYER. *Lord Jesus, help us to prepare for your return with a spirit of joyful hope.*

HE Antichrist's deception already begins to take shape in the world every time the claim is made to realize within history that messianic hope which can only be realized beyond history through the eschatological judgment.

—No. 676

MAR. 30

REFLECTION. All people long for a solution to the evils that beset our world. When Christians keep their focus on Christ and look beyond this world to things above, they are protected from the false hopes and the lies of the devil.

PRAYER. *Father, help us to keep our eyes fixed on Jesus, like a light shining in a dark world.*

† 1 Jn 2:18; cf. 1 Pet 4:7.

HEN he comes at the end of time to judge the living and the dead, the glorious Christ will reveal the secret disposition of hearts and will render to each man according to his works and according to his acceptance or refusal of grace.

—No. 682

MAR. 31

REFLECTION. We live in an age when tolerance is considered a virtue, but let us not forget that there remains One who does have the right to judge and will do so at the end of time.

PRAYER. *Lord, in your mercy, deal gently with the creatures you have created.*

Y virtue of our Baptism, the first sacrament of the faith, the Holy Spirit in the Church communicates to us, intimately and personally, the life that originates in the Father and is offered to us in the Son. —No. 683

APR. 1

REFLECTION. Each Person of the Trinity has distinct functions, and yet their unity is such that these functions are carried out in perfect cooperation, in an utter harmony that is rarely, if ever, experienced in human collaborations.

PRAYER. *God of unity, help us in our efforts to collaborate with your grace and with our fellow man.*

THE Holy Spirit is at work with the Father and the Son from the beginning to the completion of the plan for our salvation. But in these "end times" ushered in by the Son's redeeming Incarnation, the Spirit is revealed and given, recognized and welcomed as a person. —No. 686

APR. 2

REFLECTION. God never changes. But as we see him in a linear fashion, through time, he has revealed himself more and more until these "end times" when he has revealed himself most fully.

PRAYER. *Triune God, help us to know you as you really are, not as we have imagined you.*

THE Church, a communion living in the faith of the apostles which she transmits, is the place where we know the Holy Spirit. —No. 688

APR. 3

REFLECTION. The Holy Spirit speaks in the Church in many ways, primarily through Scripture, and then in Tradition, in the teaching of the Magisterium, through the sacred liturgy and prayer, as well as in each individual, through the People of God.

PRAYER. *Father, may our minds be tuned to the channels and the chosen instruments through which your Spirit speaks to us each day.*

JUST as the gestation of our first birth took place in water, so the water of Baptism truly signifies that our birth in the divine life is given to us in the Holy Spirit. —No. 694

APR. 4

REFLECTION. The most basic elements of human life are often the actual tools that God uses in our relationship with him. Water is one such element God has used—from the flood, to the Red Sea, to the Jordan river.

PRAYER. *Father, you have made all things with us in mind. May we recognize these signs of your love in creation.*

WHILE water signifies birth and the fruitfulness of life given in the Holy Spirit, fire symbolizes the transforming energy of the Holy Spirit's actions . . . who transforms what he touches. —No. 696

APR. 5

REFLECTION. The elements of creation are also highly symbolic of our relationship with God. When the Holy Spirit manifests itself in tongues of flame, it represents the transforming power, the light and the warmth of God's love for us.

PRAYER. *Father, send the fire of your spirit deep within us to transform our lives and to conform them to you.*

ARY, the all-holy ever-virgin Mother of God, is the masterwork of the mission of the Son and the Spirit in the fullness of time. —No. 721

APR. 6

REFLECTION. From the moment of the Incarnation, the Son and the Spirit work together to bring about our redemption. At that moment, Mary is made Spouse of the Holy Spirit and Mother of God, a double honor unique in all of creation.

PRAYER. *Holy Mary, Mother of God and Spouse of the Holy Spirit, pray for us sinners, now and at the hour of our death.*

ESUS does not reveal the Holy Spirit fully, until he himself has been glorified through his Death and Resurrection. —No. 728

APR. 7

REFLECTION. God has put humanity on a "need to know" basis. Although God is eternally triune, he waited until the "fullness of time" to reveal his Son, and only in these "last days" revealed and sent the Holy Spirit to be our helper.

PRAYER. *Holy Spirit, fill us with the love of God and make us worthy servants of his Son Jesus.*

"GOD is Love"† and love is his first gift, containing all others. "God's love has been poured into our hearts through the Holy Spirit who has been given to us."†† —No. 733

APR. 8

REFLECTION. Everyone who has been given the breath of life has been given a puzzle to solve. To live well and happily is a mystery we try to unravel daily. Love is the answer that solves the mystery of life and unlocks the door to joy.

PRAYER. *Father, pour out your Spirit upon us that we may live in the light of your love.*

THE mission of Christ and the Holy Spirit is brought to completion in the Church, which is the Body of Christ and the Temple of the Holy Spirit. —No. 737

APR. 9

REFLECTION. The joint mission of the Son and Holy Spirit can be seen writ large in the Church. In its mystical perfection, the Church is the continuing Incarnation of the Son, and the ongoing Pentecost of the Holy Spirit.

PRAYER. *Lord, by the working of the Holy Spirit, purify your Bride, the Church, and make her worthy of your love.*

† 1 Jn 4:8, 16.
†† Rom 5:5.

FROM the beginning to the end of time, whenever God sends his Son, he always sends his Spirit: their mission is conjoined and inseparable. —No. 743

APR. 10

REFLECTION. Deep in the human psyche is the notion of pairs, from Adam and Eve, to Noah's ark, to the disciples being sent by twos, right up to the modern hero with his obligatory sidekick. So the Father sent his Son with the Holy Spirit. Together they complete the mission of our salvation.

PRAYER. *Father, let your Son and the Holy Spirit enter our hearts and change our lives.*

THE Church has no other light than Christ's; according to a favorite image of the Church Fathers, the Church is like the moon, all its light reflected from the sun. —No. 748

APR. 11

REFLECTION. The Church has a single, simple message—to proclaim Jesus Christ. As long as the Church, and all her members, stay true to this mission we will remain a bright reflection of our Savior and give much needed light to a world in darkness.

PRAYER. *Jesus, shine your light upon the Church that she may reflect your love to all who seek you.*

IN the Church, God is "calling together" his people from all the ends of the earth. The equivalent Greek term *Kyriake,* from which the English word *Church* and the German *Kirche* are derived, means "what belongs to the Lord." —No. 751

APR. 12

REFLECTION. God has created everything that exists, and in a very real sense he owns it all. But in the Church we find a people who are peculiarly his own, set aside to be his chosen instruments of salvation and grace.

PRAYER. *Lord, may we never forget the dignity and responsibility of being called a Christian.*

GOD created the world for the sake of communion with his divine life, a communion brought about by the "convocation" of men in Christ, and this "convocation" is the Church. —No. 760

APR. 13

REFLECTION. God's perfect will desires that all things be in total communion with him, yet our free will allows us to accept or reject God's offer. In the Church we find those who have answered Christ's call to full and perfect unity with God.

PRAYER. *Father, strengthen the bonds by which the Church is united to you.*

THE gathering together of the People of God began at the moment when sin destroyed the communion of men with God, and that of men among themselves. The gathering together of the Church is, as it were, God's reaction to the chaos provoked by sin. —No. 761

APR. 14

REFLECTION. Before the fall, all things were in communion with God. But in this fallen world, it is only through the Church that creatures can obtain full and real communion with their Creator.

PRAYER. *Father, give us the grace to be in full communion with your Church and to remain there until death.*

TO fulfill the Father's will, Christ ushered in the Kingdom of heaven on earth. The Church "is the Reign of Christ already present in mystery."† —No. 763

APR. 15

REFLECTION. It is easy—and popular—to think of the Church only in terms of her mistakes, and she has many, due to our human condition. And yet, the positive effect that the Church has had on humanity is so pervasive and comprehensive that, like daylight or electricity, it is easily overlooked.

PRAYER. *Father, let the light of your Church shine before the world that you may be glorified in her works.*

† LG 3.

HE Church's first purpose is to be the sacrament of the *inner union of men with God.* Because men's communion with one another is rooted in that union with God, the Church is also the sacrament of the *unity of the human race.* —No. 775

APR. 16

REFLECTION. The universal Church touches people of every race and nation and brings them together. In the common liturgy of the Church, the world prays together. Through the Church year, the world celebrates, fasts, and mourns together.

PRAYER. *Father, may the Church give you glory from the rising of the sun to its setting.*

HE People of God is marked by characteristics that clearly distinguish it from all other religious, ethnic, political, or cultural groups found in history. —No. 782

APR. 17

REFLECTION. What distinguishes Christians from other groups? It's not their dress, their race, the way they talk, or their cuisine. It is how they love each other, the way they support the weakest, and their reverence for God.

PRAYER. *Father, may all the world know that we are Christians by our love for each other.*

FOR the Christian, "to reign is to serve [Christ]," particularly when serving "the poor and the suffering, in whom the Church recognizes the image of her poor and suffering founder."† —No. 786

APR. 18

REFLECTION. The great saints have always burned with a passion for the poor. It is their desire to see and touch Christ that has led the holiest hearts to work with the poor, for there Christ is present with great immediacy.

PRAYER. *Lord, help us to see you in the poor, and to serve you by doing good to the least of our brothers.*

[JESUS] proclaimed a mysterious and real communion between his own body and ours: "He who eats my flesh and drinks my blood abides in me, and I in him."†† —No. 787

APR. 19

REFLECTION. Catholics hold a great reverence for Christ in the Eucharist. But that solemn reverence should extend to our own bodies and to our fellow Catholics as well. In communion, we partake of the divine nature, and become one with the host we reverence.

PRAYER. *Jesus Christ, help me to honor you in me, and in my neighbor.*

† LG 8; cf. 36.
†† Jn 6:56.

THE comparison of the Church with the body casts light on the intimate bond between Christ and his Church. Not only is she gathered *around him*; she is united *in him*, in his body. —No. 789

APR. 20

REFLECTION. Keep in mind that we are not only Christians, we *are* Christ. This is why knowing Christ is so important, for only when we come to a deep relationship with Christ do we come into contact with our true selves as we were meant to be.

PRAYER. *Lord, in knowing you, may we come to know ourselves better.*

THE Spirit is the soul, as it were, of the Mystical Body, the source of its life, of its unity in diversity, and of the riches of its gifts and charisms. —No. 809

APR. 21

REFLECTION. The body of Christ is animated by the Holy Spirit. We Christians are the body of Christ only insofar as we too are animated by the Holy Spirit alive in us.

PRAYER. *Come, Holy Spirit, and fill the hearts of the faithful that they may be truly united to Christ, their head.*

IT is Christ who, through the Holy Spirit, makes his Church one, holy, catholic, and apostolic, and it is he who calls her to realize each of these qualities. —No. 811

APR. 22

REFLECTION. People form groups and gather themselves into communities for many different reasons. When people go to their local church or participate in parish activities, there is only one reason, one motivation, and one source of inspiration or accomplishment, and that is Christ.

PRAYER. *Jesus, bless our parish community and by your presence make us worthy of your name.*

SIN and the burden of its consequences constantly threaten the gift of unity. And so, the Apostle has to exhort Christians to "maintain the unity of the Spirit in the bond of peace."† —No. 814

APR. 23

REFLECTION. Unity is not an option or a goal, but in Christ it is a cosmic reality. When Christians become separated at the human level, it is a conscious and difficult process! It is not the work of the Spirit to separate and divide the Church.

PRAYER. *Father, may the Spirit inspire in us a deep longing for the unity of all Christians.*

† Eph 4:3.

APR. 24

"LL who have been justified by faith in Baptism are incorporated into Christ; they therefore have a right to be called Christians, and with good reason are accepted as brothers in the Lord by the children of the Catholic Church."† —No. 818

REFLECTION. Our love for God often leads us to proclaim and defend the Catholic Church with a triumphant zeal that can be offensive and hurtful to our Christian brothers and sisters. A commitment to Christ-like love for other denominations is essential to Christian unity.

PRAYER. *Father, help me to love my Christian neighbor as myself.*

APR. 25

HE desire to recover the unity of all Christians is a gift of Christ and a call of the Holy Spirit.†† —No. 820

REFLECTION. Christ desires all Christians to be united, and the Holy Spirit wants to lead us in that direction. A return to full Christian unity will require us to soften our hearts toward each other, spend time together, learn about each other, dialogue openly, and most importantly, pray together.

PRAYER. *Spirit of unity and peace, soften our hearts to reach out to our Christian brothers and sisters.*

† UR 3 § 1.
†† Cf. UR 1.

ALL members of the Church, including her ministers, must acknowledge that they are sinners.† —No. 827

APR. 26

REFLECTION. What could be more difficult than living in the constant tension of striving to be holy, but admitting that we are sinners? It is a tightrope walk between arrogance and discouragement. The virtues of faith, hope, and love show us the middle way and the best way.

PRAYER. *Father of all truth, help us to see ourselves as we truly are, and to rise above the limits of our human condition.*

BY *canonizing* some of the faithful, i.e., by solemnly proclaiming that they practiced heroic virtue and lived in fidelity to God's grace, the Church recognizes the power of the Spirit of holiness within her and sustains the hope of believers by proposing the saints to them as models and intercessors.†† —No. 828

APR. 27

REFLECTION. We all know the power of a good (or bad) example. In the saints, we find not only role models, but friends and helpers who assist us by their prayers.

PRAYER. *Dear patron saint, and all you saints of God, pray for us.*

† Cf. Jn 1:8-10.

†† Cf. LG 40; 48-51.

HEN she delves into her own mystery, the Church, the People of God in the New Covenant, discovers her link with the Jewish People.† —No. 839

APR. 28

REFLECTION. It is a great embarrassment and tragedy to think of Christians being involved in anti-Semitism when in fact our salvation is so intimately bound up with God's first covenant people, whose very identity Christ chose for himself in his Incarnation.

PRAYER. *Jesus, Son of David, give me a special love for people of your race, my Jewish brothers and sisters.*

"

HE plan of salvation also includes those who acknowledge the Creator, in the first place amongst whom are the Muslims; these profess to hold the faith of Abraham, and together with us they adore the one, merciful God, mankind's judge on the last day."†† —No. 841

APR. 29

REFLECTION. When we look at Muslims we see much that is good: a deep reverence for the God of Abraham, their dedication to prayer and self-sacrifice, and their desire to serve God with their entire lives.

PRAYER. *Father, salvation belongs to you alone. Be merciful when you judge my neighbor and my enemy.*

† Cf. NA 4.
†† LG 16; cf. NA 3.

THE Catholic Church recognizes in other religions that search, among shadows and images, for the God who is unknown yet near since he gives life and breath and all things and wants all men to be saved. —No. 843

APR. 30

REFLECTION. We can separate humanity into two camps. There are those who believe in some form of deity and who search for God honestly. These are fellow travelers with us, whatever their religion, in whom God is already at work.

PRAYER. *Lord, help us to recognize your Holy Spirit at work in all people.*

TO reunite all his children, scattered and led astray by sin, the Father willed to call the whole of humanity together into his Son's Church. The Church is the place where humanity must rediscover its unity and salvation. The Church is "the world reconciled."† —No. 845

MAY 1

REFLECTION. The Catholic Church is the largest organization in the world—over a billion people; and the oldest—over 2000 years. Even so, it is still a long way from its ultimate destiny to "encompass the whole of humanity."

PRAYER. *Jesus, make your Church the vehicle of grace for all of humanity.*

† St. Augustine, *Serm.* 96, 7, 9: PL 38, 588.

"Y reason of their special vocation it belongs to the laity to seek the kingdom of God by engaging in temporal affairs and directing them according to God's will."†

—No. 898

MAY 2

REFLECTION. Many factors go into choosing a career. Alongside issues of salary, location, and personal fulfillment, it should also be asked how one will seek God in this chosen line of work and in what manner one will direct that work according to God's will.

PRAYER. *Father, bless the work of our hands that it may honor you and give you glory.*

[HE laity's] activity in ecclesial communities is so necessary that, for the most part, the apostolate of the pastors cannot be fully effective without it.††

—No. 900

MAY 3

REFLECTION. Everyone talks about the priest shortage, but what about the laity shortage? The failure to participate in Sunday Mass and Parish life by "non-practicing" Catholics constitutes another sort of crisis, one that seriously hampers the work of the priests we do have.

PRAYER. *Lord, may all the baptized hear and know your voice and seek you in the community of the faithful.*

† LG 31 § 2.
†† Cf. LG 33.

"ENCE the laity, dedicated as they are to Christ and anointed by the Holy Spirit, are marvellously called and prepared so that even richer fruits of the Spirit may be produced in them."†

—No. 901

MAY 4

REFLECTION. Gone are the days when Christians believed that only priests and religious were meant to pursue a holy life. Indeed, the *Catechism* suggests that by virtue of the gifts given them, the laity are perhaps even better suited to bear spiritual fruit.

PRAYER. *Father of all the faithful, strengthen the faith of the laity.*

"LL [the laity's] works, prayers, and apostolic undertakings, family and married life, daily work, relaxation of mind and body, if they are accomplished in the Spirit . . . all these become spiritual sacrifices acceptable to God through Jesus Christ."††

—No. 901

MAY 5

REFLECTION. Catholics learn from an early age to "offer up" their trials and sufferings, but in truth, every action of our lives can and should be "offered up" to God.

PRAYER. *Father, may every area of our lives be a pleasing sacrifice to you.*

† LG 34; cf. LG 10; 1 Pet 2:5.
†† LG 34; cf. LG 10; 1 Pet 2:5.

"ND so, worshipping everywhere by their holy actions, the laity consecrate the world itself to God, everywhere offering worship by the holiness of their lives."† —No. 901

MAY 6

REFLECTION. Christians hold the power to sanctify their corner of the world simply by living a holy life. Like a sort of spiritual Midas, everything they touch, all that they influence, becomes consecrated to God.

PRAYER. *Father, never let us forget the power of holiness to change the world.*

AY people also fulfill their prophetic mission by evangelization, "that is, the proclamation of Christ by word and the testimony of life."†† —No. 905

MAY 7

REFLECTION. Telling the world about Christ happens in two ways—by word, but also by the witness of our lives. Who we are and how we act send a message more powerfully than any words we speak.

PRAYER. *Christ, may we have the grace to model our lives on the example you left for us by your time on earth.*

† LG 34; cf. LG 10; 1 Pet 2:5.
†† LG 35 § 1.

MAY 8

"N every temporal affair [the laity] are to be guided by a Christian conscience, since no human activity, even of the temporal order, can be withdrawn from God's dominion."† —No. 912

REFLECTION. As the very notion of privacy is threatened by technology which can record and retrieve every conversation, every e-mail, every action it seems, so we get a glimpse of the kind of total access God has always had to our lives. Nothing is hidden from him.

PRAYER. *Father, may we never stop thinking of you, just as you never stop thinking of us.*

MAY 9

IDDEN from eyes of men, the life of the hermit is a silent preaching of the Lord, to whom he has surrendered his life simply because he is everything to him. Here is a particular call to find in the desert, in the thick of spiritual battle, the glory of the Crucified One. —No. 921

REFLECTION. All Christians can benefit from periodic practice of the disciplines of the hermit's life: solitude, silence, withdrawal from public life, and intense prayer.

PRAYER. *Lord, may the pattern of our lives allow us to hear you speaking in the depths of our hearts.*

† LG 36 § 4.

FROM the outset of the work of evangelization, the missionary "planting" and expansion of the Church require the presence of the religious life in all its forms.† —No. 927

MAY 10

REFLECTION. Ours is an age of diversity and inclusiveness, but the Church, from her very beginnings, has always provided a multitude of ways to serve God—lay and consecrated, active, contemplative, in the city or in the desert, in community or in solitude.

PRAYER. *Father, may your spirit equip us to serve you according to our state of life.*

"**S**INCE all the faithful form one body, the good of each is communicated to the others. . . . We must therefore believe that there exists a communion of goods in the Church."†† —No. 947

MAY 11

REFLECTION. There is absolutely no cause for envy among Christians, for all blessings are shared in common. As members of Christ's body, we each have a share of the grace, the talent, and the goodness of the other—and of Christ's own attributes as well.

PRAYER. *Father, may the merits and the prayers of the saints bring us your constant help and protection.*

† Cf. AG 18; 40.
†† St. Thomas Aquinas, *Symb.*, 10.

"EVERYTHING the true Christian has is to be regarded as a good possessed in common with everyone else."†—No. 952

MAY 12

REFLECTION. An ancient Christian writer counsels, "Say of nothing, 'This is mine.'" Christian stewardship is ever mindful of the fact that everything we possess has been given to us, and could be taken back from us at any minute.

PRAYER. *Lord, give us a firm faith in you that we may be generous givers sharing freely and joyfully.*

IN this solidarity with all men, living or dead, which is founded on the communion of the saints, the least of our acts done in charity redounds to the profit of all. Every sin harms this communion. —No. 953

MAY 13

REFLECTION. Environmentalists rightly speak of the interdependence of the human family, but the consequences of this truth go far beyond pollution and deforestation and encompass the moral and spiritual life of every human being alive or dead.

PRAYER. *Father, may our lives redound to your glory and bring light and joy to the human family.*

† *Roman Catechism* I, 10, 27.

"XACTLY as Christian communion among our fellow pilgrims brings us closer to Christ, so our communion with the saints joins us to Christ, from whom as from its fountain and head issues all grace and the life of the People of God itself."†—No. 957

MAY 14

REFLECTION. The intimate unity of all creatures—living and dead—is a natural and undeniable consequence of the fact that we are in Christ and Christ is "all in all."

PRAYER. *Jesus, be everything to me as I give all that I am to you.*

"FTER her Son's Ascension, Mary "aided the beginnings of the Church by her prayers."†† In her association with the apostles and several women, "we also see Mary by her prayers imploring the gift of the Spirit, who had already overshadowed her in the Annunciation."††† —No. 965

MAY 15

REFLECTION. Mary doesn't show up often in Scripture, but at the two main actions of the Holy Spirit—the Annunciation and Pentecost—our mother is there to facilitate God's new and more intimate union with the human family.

PRAYER. *Mary, pray that the power of the Most High will overshadow us, and send his Spirit upon the Church.*

† LG 50; cf. Eph 4:1-6.
†† LG 69.
††† LG 59.

THE Apostles' Creed associates faith in the forgiveness of sins not only with faith in the Holy Spirit, but also with faith in the Church and in the communion of saints. —No. 976

MAY 16

REFLECTION. Sin and forgiveness seem so personal, and yet they are both extremely social realities, touching every member of Christ's body. This is why we must confess our sins to and receive forgiveness from the priest who represents the Body of Christ.

PRAYER. *Father, renew in your Church a deep longing for the graces you hold out to us in the sacrament of Reconciliation.*

IN this battle against our inclination towards evil, who could be brave and watchful enough to escape every wound of sin? —No. 979

MAY 17

REFLECTION. Forgiveness and reconciliation are powerful sources of healing to the human spirit and psyche, but in order to receive their benefits we must admit our sins and explicitly ask for pardon. The stage for this beautiful and necessary human drama is the confessional.

PRAYER. *Father, draw your wandering children back to you. May we embrace the healing and strength you offer us through the sacrament of Reconciliation.*

THERE is no offense, however serious, that the Church cannot forgive. . . . Christ who died for all men desires that in his Church the gates of forgiveness should always be open to anyone who turns away from sin.† —No. 982

MAY 18

REFLECTION. The sacrament of Reconciliation predates psychology, psychiatry, and psychotherapy and, as a divine grace and a gift of God, can be quite effective in its own right for inner healing, as those who frequently receive it are well aware.

PRAYER. *Lord, draw us into perfect union with you through the sacrament of Reconciliation.*

THE Christian Creed . . . culminates in the proclamation of the resurrection of the dead on the last day and in life everlasting. —No. 988

MAY 19

REFLECTION. When the first Christians chose the title "good news" to describe the story of Jesus, we might wonder what it was that made it so good. This conquering death, this sweeping away of our biggest fear is the sweet and powerful element of the story of Christ that puts the "good" in "good news."

PRAYER. *Lord Jesus, in your dying you conquered death. Let this truth be our hope.*

† Cf. Mt 18:21-22.

MAY 20

E firmly believe, and hence we hope that, just as Christ is truly risen from the dead and lives for ever, so after death the righteous will live for ever with the risen Christ and he will raise them up on the last day.† —No. 989

REFLECTION. It is not easy to "firmly believe" in the resurrection of the dead, and yet, if Christ did not rise from the dead, then we do not rise from the dead, in which case our faith is a joke and we are pathetic—as Paul himself pointed out.††

PRAYER. *Lord, we do believe, but help and heal our unbelief.*

MAY 21

OPE in the bodily resurrection of the dead established itself as a consequence intrinsic to faith in God as creator of the whole man, soul and body. —No. 992

REFLECTION. Looking around at creation and all its glory and beauty and its culmination in the human form, it is clear that God likes matter and, indeed, loves everything he has created. Why, then, would he not resurrect our bodies along with our souls?

PRAYER. *Father, help us to love our bodies because you love them and have an eternal plan for them.*

† Cf. Jn 6:39-40.

†† 1 Cor 15:13.

JESUS links faith in the resurrection to his own person: "I am the Resurrection and the life."† It is Jesus himself who on the last day will raise up those who have believed in him, who have eaten his body and drunk his blood.†† —No. 994

MAY 22

REFLECTION. We rise from the dead with Christ. Participation in the Eucharist makes this fact a necessity. When we ingest his body and blood we become one in Christ. If he rises, we rise.

PRAYER. *Lord, we believe that in rising, you restored our life and destroyed our death.*

CHRIST will raise us up "on the last day"; but it is also true that, in a certain way, we have already risen with Christ. —No. 1002

MAY 23

REFLECTION. The life of the Christian is "already but not yet." The work of Christ on our behalf is finished and in so many ways we experience that victory, but our earthly trials continue to bring us to our knees. We live with one foot on earth and one in heaven.

PRAYER. *Jesus, help us to move beyond the limits of this earthly life to experience, even now, the graces you have won for us.*

† Jn 11:25.
†† Cf. Jn 5:24-25; 6:40, 54.

EATH seems like the normal end of life. That aspect of death lends urgency to our lives: remembering our mortality helps us to realize that we have only a limited time in which to bring our lives to fulfillment. —No. 1007

MAY 24

REFLECTION. To honestly accept the fact that our days are numbered; to think about the date on which you will no longer be living; to wrestle with the reality of death, judgment, heaven, and hell is an extremely practical way to live.

PRAYER. *Lord, help us to face how fragile and finite our life really is.*

HAT is essentially new about Christian death is this: through Baptism, the Christian has already "died with Christ" sacramentally, in order to live a new life; and if we die in Christ's grace, physical death completes this "dying with Christ" and so completes our incorporation into him in his redeeming act. —No. 1010

MAY 25

REFLECTION. For the Christian, death and eternal life begin at Baptism, and they work themselves out side by side throughout our entire lives.

PRAYER. *Lord, help us to stay close to you, for all our time is tied up with the reality of you.*

EATH is the end of man's earthly pilgrimage, of the time of grace and mercy which God offers him so as to work out his earthly life in keeping with the divine plan, and to decide his ultimate destiny. . . . There is no "reincarnation" after death. —No. 1013

MAY 26

REFLECTION. For the Christian, death is the end of all chances. The buzzer sounds. Time's up. Pencils down. It's like sudden death overtime in the playoffs. When it's over, it's really over. What could be more inspirational than the mere fact that this might be the case?

PRAYER. *Lord, help us make the most of what you have given us.*

HIS perfect life with the Most Holy Trinity—this communion of life and love with the Trinity, with the Virgin Mary, the angels and all the blessed—is called "heaven." Heaven is the ultimate end and fulfillment of the deepest human longings, the state of supreme, definitive happiness. —No. 1024

MAY 27

REFLECTION. We often think of heaven as endless physical gratification, but it is more like coming home after a long day to find everyone in a good mood, the house clean, and the smell of a delicious meal cooking.

PRAYER. *Father, thank you for the gift of family and the blessings they bring.*

LL who die in God's grace and friendship, but still imperfectly purified, are indeed assured of their eternal salvation; but after death they undergo purification, so as to achieve the holiness necessary to enter the joy of heaven. —No. 1030

MAY 28

REFLECTION. Purgatory may feel like a punishment, but it is really a tremendous gift God gives us to prepare for that divine meeting, in the same way that we spend time getting ready to go out so that we will look our best and feel good about ourselves.

PRAYER. *God bless the poor souls in purgatory.*

O die in mortal sin without repenting and accepting God's merciful love means remaining separated from him for ever by our own free choice. This state of definitive self-exclusion from communion with God and the blessed is called "hell." —No. 1033

MAY 29

REFLECTION. Hell is a choice. Just as heaven is about togetherness, hell is a choice of self over God and self over others—a choice of isolation over belonging.

PRAYER. *Lord, help us to choose life, and to choose you who are the way, the truth, and the life.*

N the presence of Christ, who is Truth itself, the truth of each man's relationship with God will be laid bare.† The Last Judgment will reveal even to its furthest consequences the good each person has done or failed to do during his earthly life. —No. 1039

MAY 30

REFLECTION. It is easy to pass judgment on ourselves and other people, but these judgments pale beside Christ's final word on our lives because he can see "the furthest consequence" of all we have done or failed to do.

PRAYER. *Jesus, give me wisdom to consider the results of all I think and say.*

[
T the end of time] the beatific vision, in which God opens himself in an inexhaustible way to the elect, will be the ever-flowing well-spring of happiness, peace, and mutual communion. —No. 1045

MAY 31

REFLECTION. This is heaven: total access to God in mutual self-giving that is overflowing with happiness and peace. Not a series of ups and downs, but a sustained joy like we've never experienced before.

PRAYER. *Father, may all our earthly joys be pure and healthy and inspire us to strive more boldly for the promise of heaven.*

† Cf. Jn 12:49.

HE word "liturgy" originally meant a "public work" or a "service in the name of/on behalf of the people." In Christian tradition it means the participation of the People of God in "the work of God."† —No. 1069

JUNE 1

REFLECTION. To sit in the pew passively daydreaming during Mass is like a soccer player standing around on the soccer field, oblivious of the game going on around her, and then later saying, "I got nothing out of it."

PRAYER. *Father, thank you for the opportunity to worship you at Mass.*

"HE liturgy is the summit toward which the activity of the Church is directed; it is also the font from which all her power flows."†† —No. 1074

JUNE 2

REFLECTION. The importance of attending Church each Sunday with a community of other believers cannot be understated. It is the very essence of Christian life. To omit this one practice is to compromise the validity of your entire spiritual life.

PRAYER. *Lord, give us a deep love for and desire to embrace the Third Commandment.*

† Cf. Jn 17:4.
†† SC 10.

ROM the beginning until the end of time the whole of God's work is a *blessing.* From the liturgical poem of the first creation to the canticles of the heavenly Jerusalem, the inspired authors proclaim the plan of salvation as one vast divine blessing. —No. 1079

JUNE 3

REFLECTION. It is not always easy to admit it, but every circumstance of our lives contains the mark of a loving and gracious God who guides human affairs. He truly has the whole world in his hands.

PRAYER. *Lord, help me to turn and to return to you in every moment of my life.*

N the Church's liturgy the divine blessing is fully revealed and communicated. The Father is acknowledged and adored as the source and the end of all the blessings of creation and salvation. —No. 1082

JUNE 4

REFLECTION. The Catholic Mass is a dense and richly layered experience during which we are showered with unfiltered expressions of God's deep love for us, especially in His Word, and the Eucharistic banquet.

PRAYER. *Thank you, Father, for your great love which surpasses even our deepest and truest longings.*

JUNE 5

[HRIST'S] Paschal mystery is a real event that occurred in our history, but it is unique; all other historical events happen once, then pass away, swallowed up in the past. The Paschal mystery of Christ, by contrast . . . participates in the divine eternity, and so transcends all times while being made present in them all. —No. 1085

REFLECTION. God dwells outside of time, but entered time as a man. The Church understands the Paschal mystery we celebrate at Mass as abiding somewhere between linear time and the eternal now.

PRAYER. *Lord, fill every moment of my life with a knowledge of your presence.*

JUNE 6

"[N the earthly liturgy,] with all the warriors of the heavenly army, we sing a hymn of glory to the Lord; venerating the memory of the saints, we hope for some part and fellowship with them. "† —No. 1090

REFLECTION. We are not alone at Mass, We are joined by the angels and the saints—or, more appropriately, we join them—as they eternally and unceasingly praise the God of the Universe.

PRAYER. *All holy men and women, pray for us as we join you in worshipping the Father.*

† SC 8; cf. LG 50.

THE Church, especially during Advent and Lent and above all during the Easter Vigil, re-reads and re-lives the great events of salvation history in the "today" of her liturgy. —No. 1095

JUNE 7

REFLECTION. The liturgy celebrates God's saving activity of the past, which is essentially the same as his present behavior. God is always/still saving mankind and intervening in history. In the liturgical celebration, past and present meet in God's ever-present "today."

PRAYER. *Father, your love is unchanging and your faithfulness never fails. Accept our praise this day.*

THE Holy Spirit first recalls the meaning of the salvation event to the liturgical assembly by giving life to the Word of God, which is proclaimed so that it may be received and lived. —No. 1100

JUNE 8

REFLECTION. The reading of the Bible in all its solemnity during the Mass is like no other literary event. The Holy Spirit inhabits the words and he works from within them and from within our own spirits to make the Word bear fruit in us.

PRAYER. *Come, Holy Spirit, and enkindle a fire within our hearts through the reading of the Scriptures.*

HRISTIAN liturgy not only recalls the events that saved us but actualizes them, makes them present. The Paschal mystery of Christ is celebrated, not repeated. It is the celebrations that are repeated, and in each celebration there is an outpouring of the Holy Spirit that makes the unique mystery present. —No. 1104

JUNE 9

REFLECTION. The union between God and his creatures during the Eucharistic liturgy is so intimate that it is difficult to describe the communion of the temporal and the eternal using standard linear notions of time.

PRAYER. *Lord, inspire in us to enter deeply into the celebration of the liturgy.*

HE most intimate cooperation of the Holy Spirit and the Church is achieved in the liturgy. —No. 1108

JUNE 10

REFLECTION. We've all sensed the Holy Spirit at work in our lives individually, in a stunning coincidence, a providential meeting, or a unique relationship. In a much more profound way, but one that's easy to miss, the Holy Spirit works in and through the Church during Mass and other liturgical celebrations to create an act of worship that is pleasing and acceptable to God.

PRAYER. *Come, Holy Spirit, and kindle in the hearts of the faithful your divine fire of love.*

"HE grace of the Lord Jesus Christ and the love of God and the fellowship of the Holy Spirit"† have to remain with us always and bear fruit beyond the Eucharistic celebration. —No. 1109

JUNE 11

REFLECTION. The word "mass" comes from a Latin word for "sent," the idea being that we are sent away to live what we have prayed during the Mass. All that goes on during the liturgy is meant to equip us and strengthen us for all that goes on outside of the liturgy.

PRAYER. *Here I am, Lord; I come to do your will.*

HE law of prayer is the law of faith: the Church believes as she prays. Liturgy is a constitutive element of the holy and living Tradition.†† —No. 1124

JUNE 12

REFLECTION. Those who choose not to participate in formal liturgical celebrations are starving their faith of one of its most important sources. Our faith flows from our prayer. If our faith is to be part of the greater world of reality, so our worship and prayer must enter into the public life of the Church.

PRAYER. *Lord, inspire all Christians to return to the active practice of their faith.*

† 2 Cor 13:13.
†† Cf. DV 8.

THE fruits of the sacraments also depend on the disposition of the one who receives them. —No. 1128

JUNE 13

REFLECTION. In the parable of the sower, Jesus describes the way that seeds take to different types of soil. It is our responsibility to prepare the soil of our hearts before we come to Mass or receive the sacraments.

PRAYER. *Pray for us, Holy Mother of God, that we may be made worthy of the promises of Christ.*

LITURGY is an "action" of the *whole Christ*. . . . Those who even now celebrate it without signs are already in the heavenly liturgy, where celebration is wholly communion and feast. —No. 1136

JUNE 14

REFLECTION. The Body of Christ is made up of all the members of the Church—those living and the dead. During the Mass they are all brought together to worship Christ in a unique way, so that the Mass is ultimate experience. Christ in heaven, and Christ on earth.

PRAYER. *Lord, join all the members of your Body together in a perfect, eternal unity.*

"**MOTHER Church earnestly desires that all the faithful should be led to that full, conscious, and active participation in liturgical celebrations which is demanded by the very nature of the liturgy."†** —No. 1141

JUNE 15

REFLECTION. One of the great challenges of the Christian life is to take that one hour each week on Sunday and to give it back to God. Just having our body there can be enough of a challenge, but the Church suggests "full, conscious, and active participation."

PRAYER. *Jesus, thank you for the opportunity to attend Mass; help us to honor you by our worship.*

A SACRAMENTAL celebration is woven from signs and symbols. In keeping with the divine pedagogy of salvation, their meaning is rooted in the work of creation and in human culture . . . and fully revealed in the person and work of Christ. —No. 1145

JUNE 16

REFLECTION. The Catholic liturgy as we know it today is part of a long tradition and was developed in a time when most people could not read. For this reason it is heavy with symbolism and ritual which speak to us in a deep, subconscious way.

PRAYER. *Lord, let us see your glory in the power of signs and symbols.*

† SC 14.

In human life, signs and symbols occupy an important place. As a being at once body and spirit, man expresses and perceives spiritual realities through physical signs and symbols. —No. 1146

JUNE 17

REFLECTION. The Mass speaks to us at many levels: intellectually, through the spoken words, but also emotionally and spiritually. Candles, incense, vestments, processions, etc., all these things help us worship our Lord, for Christ is the meaning behind all of these signs.

PRAYER. *Father, may we enter more deeply into the mystery of our salvation through active participation in the Mass.*

The liturgy of the Church presupposes, integrates and sanctifies elements from creation and human culture, conferring on them the dignity of signs of grace, of the new creation in Jesus Christ. —No. 1149

JUNE 18

REFLECTION. The centrality of mundane, physical elements like water, wine, and bread in our worship reminds us that our relationship with God encompasses the whole human experience. Even at worship, maybe especially then, our relationship with God is physical as well as spiritual.

PRAYER. *Lord, sanctify every element of our world and use them to bring us closer to you.*

INCE Pentecost, it is through the sacramental signs of his Church that the Holy Spirit carries on the work of sanctification. The sacraments of the Church do not abolish but purify and integrate all the richness of the signs and symbols of the cosmos and of social life. —No. 1152

JUNE 19

REFLECTION. Each and every time that a sacrament is performed it is a sort of mini-Pentecost, a moment of growth in the Church through a new outpouring of the Holy Spirit to reconcile, strengthen, and inspire God's people.

PRAYER. *Lord, send forth your spirit and renew your Church.*

"

HE musical tradition of the universal Church is a treasure of inestimable value, greater even than that of any other art."† . . . "He who sings prays twice."†† —No. 1156

JUNE 20

REFLECTION. Melody and song have a powerful effect on human beings, touching them at the deepest physical and spiritual levels. As an aid to communion with the divine, music is the ideal combination of vulnerability, participation, self-expression, and beauty.

PRAYER. *Lord, may we use the gift of music to praise you in psalms, hymns, and inspired songs.*

† SC 112.
†† St. Augustine, *En. in Ps.* 72, 1: PL 36, 914.

[THE] sacred images of the holy Mother of God and of the saints as well . . . make manifest the "cloud of witnesses"† who continue to participate in the salvation of the world and to whom we are united, above all in sacramental celebrations. —No. 1161

JUNE 21

REFLECTION. In icons, statues, and holy cards of the saints we see our extended family brought to our memory for support and inspiration. We are reminded of their continued participation, with us, in the saving act of Christ.

PRAYER. *All you saints of God, pray for us that we may imitate your lives of devotion and service.*

SIMILARLY, the contemplation of sacred icons, united with meditation on the Word of God and the singing of liturgical hymns, enters into the harmony of the signs of celebration so that the mystery celebrated is imprinted in the heart's memory and is then expressed in the new life of the faithful.—No. 1162

JUNE 22

REFLECTION. It is okay to look around at church during Mass, particularly in a church where the architecture, statuary, and art all tell the Gospel story with beauty and clarity.

PRAYER. *Lord, inspire those whose charge it is to build churches to your glory.*

† Heb 12:1.

WHEN the Church celebrates the mystery of Christ, there is a word that marks her prayer: "Today!"—a word echoing the prayer her Lord taught her and the call of the Holy Spirit.† This "today" of the living God which man is called to enter is "the hour" of Jesus' Passover, which reaches across and underlies all history. —No. 1165

JUNE 23

REFLECTION. The Sacred Triduum of Christ's passion, death, and resurrection is a motif undergirding every day of our lives: we celebrate, we suffer, we wait, and ultimately we rejoice.

PRAYER. *Lord, open our hearts to hear your voice today.*

THE ***lectio divina,*** **where the Word of God is so read and meditated that it becomes prayer, is thus rooted in the liturgical celebration.** —No. 1177

JUNE 24

REFLECTION. The Word of God is so rich and powerful that the ancient monks devised a process of reading Scripture that was slow and meditative, taking small amounts at a time and meditating on one word or phrase throughout the day. This approach to Scripture is at the heart of the liturgy.

PRAYER. *Lord, may we open our minds and hearts to hear your Word.*

† Cf. Mt 6:11; Heb 3:7—4:11; Ps 95:7.

HE seven sacraments touch all the stages and all the important moments of Christian life:† they give birth and increase, healing and mission to the Christian's life of faith. There is thus a certain resemblance between the stages of natural life and the stages of the spiritual life. —No. 1210

JUNE 25

REFLECTION. Christ is always with us, but in the sacraments he is present powerfully and physically at our most important moments—those joyful, such as birth and marriage, and those most difficult, such as illness and death.

PRAYER. *Jesus, help us to recognize your real presence in the sacraments.*

APTISM imprints on the soul an indelible spiritual sign, the character, which consecrates the baptized person for Christian worship. —No. 1280

JUNE 26

REFLECTION. In Baptism, Christians are consecrated, that is, set apart, to serve God in worship and in service.

PRAYER. *Father, you make us in your own image, and in Baptism remake us as new creatures drawn to you in love. Help us to follow the spiritual instincts that Baptism has placed within us.*

† Cf. St. Thomas Aquinas, *STh* III, 65, 1.

THIS seal of the Holy Spirit marks our total belonging to Christ, our enrollment in his service for ever, as well as the promise of divine protection in the great eschatological trial.† —No. 1296

JUNE 27

REFLECTION. As social animals, we long to belong and we give our allegiance to this or that group. Similarly, others make claims on us and exert influence thereby. And yet, in Baptism we are given totally over to Christ, whose proprietary claim on us supersedes all other allegiances.

PRAYER. *O my God, I am completely yours. O my Jesus, enter.*

THE Eucharist is "the source and summit of the Christian life."†† —No. 1324

JUNE 28

REFLECTION. The ancients spoke of "ambrosia," this food of the gods that gave immortality to mortals if they could eat it. In the Eucharist we share not just food of the gods but food that is God. All of the power and wisdom and strength contained in the divinity of Christ becomes a part of us as we partake in the heavenly banquet.

PRAYER. *Lord, help me to come to a deeper belief and a fuller understanding of the gift you give us of yourself in the Eucharist.*

† Cf. Rev 7:2-3; 9:4; Ezek 9:4-6.
†† LG 11.

FAITHFUL to the Lord's command the Church continues to do, in his memory and until his glorious return, what he did on the eve of his Passion: "He took bread. . . ." "taking the chalice filled with the fruit of the vine. . . ." —No. 1333

JUNE 29

REFLECTION. The weekly ritual of the Mass may seem awkward or inconvenient, but unlike most of the ways in which we spend our lives, it is not a consumer's decision; it is an act of obedience to the Lord's words.

PRAYER. *Lord, may the Church always remain faithful to your words at the Last Supper.*

THE miracles of the multiplication of the loaves, when the Lord says the blessing, breaks and distributes the loaves through his disciples to feed the multitude, prefigure the superabundance of this unique bread of his Eucharist.†

—No. 1335

JUNE 30

REFLECTION. Upon finally grasping the reality of what it means to eat Jesus' body and blood, one teenager exclaimed, "It must have been a big body!" The multiplication of the loaves explains God's fecundity and how we are able to continually feed on the true body of Christ.

PRAYER. *Lord, help me to have a firmer faith in the Eucharist.*

† Cf. Mt 14:13-21; 15:32-39.

N the Eucharist, the sacrifice of Christ becomes also the sacrifice of the members of his Body. —No. 1368

JULY 1

REFLECTION. Every Christian is to be a martyr and a hero, daily sacrificing oneself for others: being kind, bearing wrongs patiently, letting go of anger, giving in, putting others above self. This type of sacrifice is pleasing to the Father and ascends to him each Sunday during the Eucharistic prayer along with the perfect sacrifice of Christ.

PRAYER. *Jesus, help us to live a life worthy of your name, and pleasing to you in every way.*

O the offering of Christ are united not only the members still here on earth, but also those already *in the glory of heaven.* In communion with and commemorating the Blessed Virgin Mary and all the saints, the Church offers the Eucharistic sacrifice. —No. 1370

JULY 2

REFLECTION. One constant theme of the *Catechism* is the unity of Christians still living on earth and those deceased in heaven. The underlying message is the clear belief that our faith transcends the limits of death.

PRAYER. *Lord, help us to draw strength from our fellow Christians in heaven—especially our own loved ones.*

N the liturgy of the Mass we express our faith in the real presence of Christ under the species of bread and wine by, among other ways, genuflecting or bowing deeply as a sign of adoration of the Lord. —No. 1378

JULY 3

REFLECTION. Physical acts of reverence are important public, outward signs of what is in our hearts. If our love for God is real, it has to manifest itself beyond interior dialogues and spill over into the physical world where so much of what we know as "reality" resides.

PRAYER. *Lord, look upon us humbly prostrate before you and hear our prayers.*

HE celebration of the Eucharistic sacrifice is wholly directed toward the intimate union of the faithful with Christ through communion. To receive communion is to receive Christ himself who has offered himself for us.

—No. 1382

JULY 4

REFLECTION. Just as marriage has a means for husband and wife to conjugate their love and fulfill their burning desire for nearness and unity, so Christ instituted the Eucharist for those who love him. We can get no nearer to him than to ingest his very body and blood.

PRAYER. *Lord, let the unity we share with you be manifest in our life.*

O respond to this invitation we must *prepare ourselves* for so great and so holy a moment. St. Paul urges us to examine our conscience: "Whoever, therefore, eats the bread or drinks the cup of the Lord in an unworthy manner will be guilty of profaning the body and blood of the Lord. . . ."† —No. 1385

JULY 5

REFLECTION. When we grasp the reality of the Eucharist, the one-hour fast seems hardly adequate preparation. Would that we spent at least an hour preparing our minds and hearts as well.

PRAYER. *Lord, never let us take the Eucharist for granted.*

HE principal fruit of receiving the Eucharist in Holy Communion is an intimate union with Christ Jesus. Indeed, the Lord said: "He who eats my flesh and drinks my blood abides in me, and I in him."†† —No. 1391

JULY 6

REFLECTION. Among a handful of themes that the *Catechism* repeats over and over again is the intimate union of the Christian with Jesus Christ and the fact that, as true members of his body, we *are* the body of Christ.

PRAYER. *Lord, help us to grow in unity with you each day.*

† 1 Cor 11:27-29.
†† Jn 6:56.

HAT material food produces in our bodily life, Holy Communion wonderfully achieves in our spiritual life. Communion with the flesh of the risen Christ, a flesh "given life and giving life through the Holy Spirit,"† preserves, increases, and renews the life of grace received at Baptism. —No. 1392

JULY 7

REFLECTION. He first appears as a baby in a manger; his parables are rich with banquet imagery; he feeds the crowds; he dines with sinners; and he calls himself the Bread of Life. Jesus clearly presents himself as food for those who believe in him.

PRAYER. *Lord, may our spirits grow strong from feeding on your body and blood.*

S bodily nourishment restores lost strength, so the Eucharist strengthens our charity, which tends to be weakened in daily life; and this living charity *wipes away venial sins.*†† —No. 1394

JULY 8

REFLECTION. Frequent reception of Holy Communion is as beneficial for our spirit as eating regularly is for our body. Christ has given his very self as bread for the journey.

PRAYER. *Body of Jesus, strengthen me; blood of Jesus, purify me.*

† PO 5.

†† Cf. Council of Trent (1551): DS 1638.

HE more painful the experience of the divisions in the Church which break the common participation in the table of the Lord, the more urgent are our prayers to the Lord that the time of complete unity among all who believe in him may return. —No. 1398

JULY 9

REFLECTION. The Church urges us not to indulge in a false unity by sharing in the Lord's Supper across denominations, thinking it is better for us to feel the pain our separation causes. This pain should stir us to work for unity all the more.

PRAYER. *Lord, hasten the day when Holy Communion is truly that.*

HRIST'S call to conversion continues to resound in the lives of Christians. This *second conversion* is an uninterrupted task for the whole Church. —No. 1428

JULY 10

REFLECTION. In addition to those radical moments of repentance and conversion, there is another gradual change that should go on continually within each Christian, a slow maturation of spirit that follows the natural course of physical, intellectual, and emotional growth.

PRAYER. *Lord, let not a day pass without some growth in my spirit.*

JULY 11

INTERIOR repentance is a radical reorientation of our whole life, a return, a conversion to God with all our heart, an end of sin, a turning away from evil, with repugnance toward the evil actions we have committed.
—No. 1431

REFLECTION. An occasional crisis in our family, career, and relationships is really a sign that these things are vibrant and growing. In the same way, our spiritual life should be punctuated with occasional crises that lead to interior conversion and repentance.

PRAYER. *Lord, give me the courage to cast out into the deep.*

JULY 12

CHRIST has willed that in her prayer and life and action his whole Church should be the sign and instrument of the forgiveness and reconciliation that he acquired for us at the price of his blood.
—No. 1442

REFLECTION. Christ created the Church as a sort of ambassador for peace, a mediator who organizes and facilitates "peace talks" between the believer and the Father. The Church is empowered by Christ to both accept our contrition and impart his forgiveness and grace.

PRAYER. *Jesus, help me to love the Church you founded as I love you.*

T HE words ***bind and loose*** mean: whomever you exclude from your communion, will be excluded from communion with God; whomever you receive anew into your communion, God will welcome back into his. ***Reconciliation with the Church is inseparable from reconciliation with God.*** —No. 1445

JULY 13

REFLECTION. The Church is the Body of Christ, and Jesus is the head. Just as it is impossible to be at peace with the head and at war with the body, so it is impossible to be at peace with Christ and estranged from the Church.

PRAYER. *Jesus, help us to separate the human from the divine in our experience of Church.*

T HE confession (or disclosure) of sins, even from a simply human point of view, frees us and facilitates our reconciliation with others. —No. 1455

JULY 14

REFLECTION. As with all the sacraments, the Sacrament of Reconciliation is founded on a basic human drive—the need to speak out the truth about our life to another human being, to ask forgiveness, to seek harmony with the ultimate source of our being.

PRAYER. *Father, draw all your children back to harmony with you through the Sacrament of Reconciliation.*

NDEED the regular confession of our venial sins helps us form our conscience, fight against evil tendencies, let ourselves be healed by Christ and progress in the life of the Spirit. —No. 1458

JULY 15

REFLECTION. There is a lot to gain from going to confession. In addition to the natural human healing—which we could very well gain in psychotherapy—there are supernatural benefits that touch the deepest spiritual places of our being.

PRAYER. *Lord, by your Spirit awaken in your Church a deep hunger for the sacramental graces of Confession.*

IVEN the delicacy and greatness of this ministry and the respect due to persons, the Church declares that every priest who hears confessions is bound under very strict penalties to keep absolute secrecy regarding the sins that his penitents have confessed to him. —No. 1467

JULY 16

REFLECTION. Some people find it very difficult to go to confession, and yet, by seeing Christ in the priest, and knowing that our secrets are safe with him, we can take advantage of this gift to unburden ourselves.

PRAYER. *Lord, remove all the obstacles that harden our hearts against your wonderful gift of forgiveness.*

EVERY sin, even venial, entails an unhealthy attachment to creatures, which must be purified either here on earth or after death in the state called Purgatory.

—No. 1472

JULY 17

REFLECTION. Daily life on earth is filled with opportunities to form attachments to things that give us short-term comfort, but which hold us back from reaching our full potential as beings who are bound for divinity. Purifying ourselves from such attachments takes a lifetime—and often longer!

PRAYER. *Lord, help us to see Purgatory as yet another sign of your prodigal love for us.*

TO the eyes of faith no evil is graver than sin and nothing has worse consequence for sinners themselves, for the Church, and for the whole world.

—No. 1488

JULY 18

REFLECTION. All pain is a trial, but pain caused by deliberate malicious actions is almost unbearable to the human psyche, because it brings, along with grief, a sense of horror and fear. And every intentional act of wrongdoing we commit, however small, spreads abroad in a cosmic way, some degree of fear and grief.

PRAYER. *Lord, by your grace and the life of your divine Son, heal the world of the pain caused by our sin.*

ILLNESS and suffering have always been among the gravest problems confronted in human life. In illness, man experiences his powerlessness, his limitations, and his finitude. Every illness can make us glimpse death. —No. 1500

JULY 19

REFLECTION. In the throes of a painful illness we are tormented with the knowledge that when we were healthy, we didn't appreciate it—hardly realizing how blessed is the state of health. This same experience will be repeated in the moment after death when we realize how much for granted we took the state of life.

PRAYER. *Lord, help us to see how short and fragile our life is!*

ILLNESS can lead to anguish, self-absorption, sometimes even despair and revolt against God. It can also make a person more mature, helping him discern in his life what is not essential so that he can turn toward that which is. Very often illness provokes a search for God and a return to him.

—No. 1501

JULY 20

REFLECTION. Central to the Christian message is the counterintuitive notion that suffering can be productive, that pain borne patiently and well can sanctify, strengthen, and redeem. This is part of what makes Christianity "good" news.

PRAYER. *Lord, put all our suffering to good use!*

JESUS has the power not only to heal, but also to forgive sins;† he has come to heal the whole man, soul and body; he is the physician the sick have need of.††

—No. 1503

JULY 21

REFLECTION. We often think of Jesus as healer only in spiritual terms, but Jesus is concerned with our whole bodies. During his time on earth he practiced a very "holistic" healing approach, healing mind and body. We must still see him this way.

PRAYER. *Jesus, be the true healer for all the suffering and sick.*

HIS preferential love for the sick has not ceased through the centuries to draw the very special attention of Christians toward all those who suffer in body and soul. It is the source of tireless efforts to comfort them.

—No. 1503

JULY 22

REFLECTION. At the bottom of our thoughts when we see a sick person is "at least it's not me," or we cover our mouths and say, "I hope it's not contagious." We must keep in mind that this was never Christ's reaction to the sick.

PRAYER. *Sacred Heart of Jesus, make our hearts like yours!*

† Cf. Mk 2:5-12.
†† Cf. Mk 2:17.

Y his passion and death on the cross Christ has given a new meaning to suffering: it can henceforth configure us to him and unite us with his redemptive Passion. —No. 1505

JULY 23

REFLECTION. Uniting ourselves to Christ is an exhilarating and costly adventure. The glory and power of his divine nature can be ours, but only if we also bear the weakness, pain, and suffering of his human life. And yet, in Christ, even suffering is powerful and glorious.

PRAYER. *Jesus, help your people to imitate you more closely in all things.*

HE Church believes and confesses that among the seven sacraments there is one especially intended to strengthen those who are being tried by illness, the Anointing of the Sick. —No. 1511

JULY 24

REFLECTION. The sacraments are the continuing presence of Christ on earth. Those of us who were not alive in first-century Palestine can still encounter the Incarnate Word in a physical way through the sacraments. In the Anointing of the Sick, Christ still walks the earth as healer.

PRAYER. *Jesus, Son of David, have mercy on me.*

TWO other sacraments, Holy Orders and Matrimony, are directed towards the salvation of others; if they contribute as well to personal salvation, it is through service to others that they do so. —No. 1534

JULY 25

REFLECTION. In Marriage the spouses minister to each other in a priestly fashion. In Holy Orders, the Priest loves the faithful with the sacrificial love of a spouse. Both states are similar in their demand to pour oneself out for others.

PRAYER. *Father, give us the courage to give ourselves totally to others.*

WHILE the common priesthood of the faithful is exercised by the unfolding of baptismal grace—a life of faith, hope, and charity, a life according to the Spirit—, the ministerial priesthood is at the service of the common priesthood. It is directed at the unfolding of the baptismal grace of all Christians.

—No. 1547

JULY 26

REFLECTION. The priest exercises in a concentrated and pure form the same priestly calling which we all receive at our Baptism. In his ministerial priesthood the priest teaches the laity how to live the common priesthood by example.

PRAYER. *Jesus, help us to live out our baptismal priesthood.*

JULY 27

"**AMONGST those various offices which have been exercised in the Church from the earliest times the chief place, according to the witness of tradition, is held by the function of those who, through their appointment to the dignity and responsibility of bishop, and in virtue consequently of the unbroken succession going back to the beginning, are regarded as transmitters of the apostolic line."†** —No. 1555

REFLECTION. Just as Christ continues to walk the earth in the sacraments, so he continues to have the help of "the twelve" in the Bishops.

PRAYER. *Lord, bless our Bishop and all the Bishops of the Church.*

JULY 28

**THROUGH the sacrament of Holy Orders priests share in the universal dimensions of the mission that Christ entrusted to the apostles.** —No. 1565

REFLECTION. As the rights and responsibilities of the twelve apostles continue in the Bishops, so also the priests carry out that great commission as helpers to the Bishops. Priests dedicate themselves in service to their Bishop and extend the ministry of the Bishop by their works and sacrifices.

PRAYER. *Father, bless our parish priest and all the priests of the Church.*

† LG 20.

MONG other tasks, it is the task of deacons to assist the bishop and priests in the celebration of the divine mysteries, above all the Eucharist, in the distribution of Holy Communion, in assisting at and blessing marriages, in the proclamation of the Gospel and preaching, in presiding over funerals, and in dedicating themselves to the various ministries of charity.† —No. 1570

JULY 29

REFLECTION. Permanent deacons take on a double dose of sacrifice as husbands and as ordained ministers, serving the Church, their families, and often their careers all at the same time. These brave and selfless men need our prayers and support every bit as much as our priests.

PRAYER. *Jesus, strengthen our parish deacon and all deacons.*

IVEN the importance that the ordination of a bishop, a priest, or a deacon has for the life of the particular Church, its celebration calls for as many of the faithful as possible to take part. —No. 1572

JULY 30

REFLECTION. Every wedding calls for—and ultimately receives—a communal celebration of some sort. The same is true of an ordination—it is the whole community's business to support, pray for, and celebrate the ordination of these servants of God.

PRAYER. *Lord, gather your people together in celebration of the ordained life.*

† Cf. LG 29; SC 35 § 4; AG 16.

THE whole Church is a priestly people. Through Baptism all the faithful share in the priesthood of Christ. This participation is called the "common priesthood of the faithful." —No. 1591

JULY 31

REFLECTION. Just as each Christian is called to identify with Christ, so each Christian is called to identify with his/her bishop, priest, and deacon. The life of the ordained is not to be considered alien to the laity, but something they understand, emulate, and share in.

PRAYER. *Jesus, unite all the functions of your body, lay and ordained, in perfect harmony.*

GOD who created man out of love also calls him to love—the fundamental and innate vocation of every human being. For man is created in the image and likeness of God who is himself love.† —No. 1604

AUG. 1

REFLECTION. Love is life—everything else is just details. Just as new life is created out of the overflow of love between a man and a woman, so all of life was and is continually created out of the overflow of the love that is the Supreme Being.

PRAYER. *Father of Love, source of every blessing, help us love as you do.*

† Cf. Gen 1:27; 1 Jn 4:8, 16.

EVERY man experiences evil around him and within himself. This experience makes itself felt in the relationships between man and woman. Their union has always been threatened by discord, a spirit of domination, infidelity, jealousy, and conflicts that can escalate into hatred and separation. —No. 1606

AUG. 2

REFLECTION. The union of a man and woman is the most natural thing in the world, and yet, it is not without its predators—most of which lie within the couple themselves, especially in the form of fear and pride.

PRAYER. *Lord, grant the grace of faith and humility to married couples.*

AS A break with God, the first sin had for its first consequence the rupture of the original communion between man and woman. —No. 1607

AUG. 3

REFLECTION. The book of Genesis is so often debated as an authority on the geological nature of the earth. We shouldn't let such a debate draw our attention from the power of this book as a rich reflection on *human* nature. Especially in the story of Adam and Eve, we stand to learn a great deal about ourselves.

PRAYER. *Holy Spirit, direct and inspire our reading of the Bible.*

THE punishments consequent upon sin, "pain in childbearing" and toil "in the sweat of your brow,"† also embody remedies that limit the damaging effects of sin. After the fall, marriage helps to overcome self-absorption, egoism, pursuit of one's own pleasure, and to open oneself to the other, to mutual aid and self-giving. —No. 1609

AUG. 4

REFLECTION. Committing your life in service to another and then begetting and raising children together is one of the surest ways to reach your full human potential. The sheer difficulty of marriage makes it a powerful remedy for our pettiness and immaturity.

PRAYER. *Jesus, give married couples the grace of perseverance.*

THE Church attaches great importance to Jesus' presence at the wedding at Cana. She sees in it the confirmation of the goodness of marriage and the proclamation that thenceforth marriage will be an efficacious sign of Christ's presence. —No. 1613

AUG. 5

REFLECTION. Though Christ did not marry, he gave marriage an important place in his ministry and teaching. He began his ministry at a wedding and often spoke of the kingdom of heaven in terms of the wedding banquet, ultimately revealing himself as the bridegroom giving himself to his bride, the Church.

PRAYER. *Jesus, give your people a deep respect for the dignity of marriage.*

† Gen 3:16, 19.

T IS by following Christ, renouncing themselves, and taking up their crosses that spouses will be able to "receive" the original meaning of marriage and live it with the help of Christ.† **—No. 1615**

AUG. 6

REFLECTION. Christ is God and didn't need us, and yet, he emptied himself and took the form of a servant—our servant—in order to redeem us and make us his own spouse. This selfless outpouring is the model for married couples to imitate.

PRAYER. *Father, give the grace of selflessness and charity to married couples.*

IRGINITY for the sake of the kingdom of heaven is an unfolding of baptismal grace, a powerful sign of the supremacy of the bond with Christ and of the ardent expectation of his return, a sign which also recalls that marriage is a reality of this present age which is passing away.†† **—No. 1619**

AUG. 7

REFLECTION. Celibacy is a human experience that is deep within our race. Every major culture in history has had a class of people among them who were vowed to virginity. These people serve as a powerful sign of the reality of a life beyond this world.

PRAYER. *Lord, help us support those vowed to celibacy for your sake.*

† Cf. Mt 19:11.
†† Cf. Mk 12:25; 1 Cor 7:31.

THE spouses as ministers of Christ's grace mutually confer upon each other the sacrament of Matrimony by expressing their consent before the Church. —No. 1623

AUG. 8

REFLECTION. The exchange of wedding vows is a time when lay Catholics administer a sacrament, when they confer the Sacrament of Marriage upon each other. This priestly, sacramental act is a sign of the way in which marriage is a ministry of service.

PRAYER. *Lord, give to married couples a heart for joyful service.*

"FROM a valid marriage arises *a bond* between the spouses which by its very nature is perpetual and exclusive; furthermore, in a Christian marriage the spouses are strengthened and, as it were, consecrated for the duties and the dignity of their state *by a special sacrament.*" † —No. 1638

AUG. 9

REFLECTION. The Sacrament of Marriage confers many supernatural graces upon a couple in recognition of the fact that a marriage lived as a lifetime of love, fidelity, and service is really beyond our natural capabilities and requires supernatural help.

PRAYER. *Lord, pour out on all married couples the fullness of sacramental graces.*

† Cf. CIC, can. 1134.

"CONJUGAL love involves a totality, in which all the elements of the person enter. . . . It aims at a deeply personal unity, a unity that, beyond union in one flesh, leads to forming one heart and soul; it demands *indissolubility* and *faithfulness* in definitive mutual giving; and it is open to *fertility*. . . ."†

—No. 1643

AUG. 10

REFLECTION. Where there is fidelity and complete openness to the possibility of new life, the conjugal act becomes the high water mark of selflessness, service, and humility for both husband and wife.

PRAYER. *Lord, give to married couples the grace of fidelity and courage.*

BY its very nature conjugal love requires the inviolable fidelity of the spouses. This is the consequence of the gift of themselves which they make to each other. Love seeks to be definitive; it cannot be an arrangement "until further notice."

—No. 1646

AUG. 11

REFLECTION. The staggering number of choices available to contemporary man makes commitment difficult. The incessant nagging sensation of what we might be missing "on the other channels" makes commitment seem like one option among many, when in fact it is the gateway to true freedom.

PRAYER. *Holy Spirit, bear in us the fruit of faithfulness.*

† FC 13.

THE fruitfulness of conjugal love extends to the fruits of the moral, spiritual, and supernatural life that parents hand on to their children by education. . . . In this sense the fundamental task of marriage and family is to be at the service of life.† —No. 1653

AUG. 12

REFLECTION. Marriage is all about life. It is the fundamental building block of a civilized society. When spouses and their children live in a mutual exchange of love and faithfulness to each other they increase the quality of life in the society they inhabit.

PRAYER. *Father, give to families the grace of unity.*

THE Christian home is the place where children receive the first proclamation of the faith. For this reason the family home is rightly called the "domestic church," a community of grace and prayer, a school of human virtues and of Christian charity. —No. 1666

AUG. 13

REFLECTION. Christians often bring a consumer mentality to their local church, when in reality they are contributors, not consumers. They build the Church first within the walls of their own home, and then bring that experience of grace and prayer to their local parish.

PRAYER. *Father, give to Christian families the grace of holiness.*

† Cf. FC 28.

"HERE is scarcely any proper use of material things which cannot be thus directed toward the sanctification of men and the praise of God."†

—No. 1670

AUG. 14

REFLECTION. In the course of a day Christians should either make holy or be made holy by everything they come in contact with. This is done simply by seeing everything in the light of our relationship with God and our neighbor. Such a viewpoint will lead us to act and speak with virtue and Christian charity.

PRAYER. *Lord, open our eyes to see you present and at work in all of creation.*

HE first and last point of reference of this catechesis will always be Jesus Christ himself, who is "the way, and the truth, and the life."†† It is by looking to him in faith that Christ's faithful can hope that he himself fulfills his promises in them. —No. 1698

AUG. 15

REFLECTION. Just as Christ stands at the middle of human history—his birth a dividing line separating that which went before him to that which came after—so he should be in our life the center point which divides his presence in us from all that is not him.

PRAYER. *Jesus, be everything to me.*

† SC 61.
†† Jn 14:6.

Y his reason, man recognizes the voice of God which urges him "to do what is good and avoid what is evil."† . . . Living a moral life bears witness to the dignity of the person. —No. 1706

AUG. 16

REFLECTION. A major part of the dignity of the human being is reason—that which separates us from the animals. When we employ our reason to work, create, bless, and heal we manifest the image of God within us.

PRAYER. *Father, help us to turn our minds to what is true, pure, and good.*

Y his Passion, Christ delivered us from Satan and from sin. He merited for us the new life in the Holy Spirit. His grace restores what sin had damaged in us. —No. 1708

AUG. 17

REFLECTION. Christ delivered us from Satan and from sin. This statement is one of those things you hear so often that you lose sight of its power. All who believe this statement should work hard to internalize it until it makes a concrete difference in their disposition.

PRAYER. *Christ, we thank you and praise you for the many ways you have cared for us.*

† GS 16.

HE Beatitudes respond to the natural desire for happiness. This desire is of divine origin: God has placed it in the human heart in order to draw man to the One who alone can fulfill it: . . . God alone satisfies.† —No. 1718

AUG. 18

REFLECTION. Most of our strongest and simplest desires drive us to do that which is good for us—such as eating, drinking, and procreation. Likewise, our desire for happiness can and should drive us to do good things, though it can be corrupted, just as when hunger and love turn into gluttony and lust.

PRAYER. *Lord, purify our hearts and fill us with holy longings.*

OD put us in the world to know, to love, and to serve him, and so to come to paradise. —No. 1721

AUG. 19

REFLECTION. These words are the answer to one of the first questions of the old *Baltimore Catechism*. It is a statement that was memorized by several generations of American Catholic schoolchildren. Such a simple and eloquent answer to the question of human existence should be assimilated by all Christians.

PRAYER. *Father, fill us with the hope of heaven and a desire for eternity with you.*

† St. Thomas Aquinas, *Expos. in symb. apost.* I.

HE Decalogue, the Sermon on the Mount, and the apostolic catechesis describe for us the paths that lead to the Kingdom of heaven. Sustained by the grace of the Holy Spirit, we tread them, step by step, by everyday acts.

—No. 1724

AUG. 20

REFLECTION. Everything counts. Nothing is neutral. We are always on. Every thought, word, and act has some influence on our eternal destiny.

PRAYER. *Lord, help us to live every moment in accordance with your will.*

REEDOM is the power, rooted in reason and will, to act or not to act, to do this or that, and so to perform deliberate actions on one's own responsibility. By free will one shapes one's own life. —No. 1731

AUG. 21

REFLECTION. One simple way to realize how radical is the freedom that God has given us is to reflect on what it means to be able to tell a lie. The mere ability to restate reality and speak of it as it is not is a powerful example of the freedom God has given us to shape our world.

PRAYER. *Jesus, help us to use our freedom in righteousness.*

UMAN freedom is a force for growth and maturity in truth and goodness; it attains its perfection when directed toward God, our beatitude. —No. 1731

AUG. 22

REFLECTION. We've all heard it said, but it bears repeating that God did not want robots who were programmed to serve him and who had no choice but to do good. It is only the ever-present option to do evil that gives merit to our good acts and makes them pleasing to God.

PRAYER. *Father, you trust us with responsibility for our own lives. Help us to make right choices in freedom.*

HE more one does what is good, the freer one becomes. There is no true freedom except in the service of what is good and just. —No. 1733

AUG. 23

REFLECTION. Sin is a hard master. Though it usually begins with exhilaration and excitement, sin often ends in bitterness and self-loathing. Righteousness, on the other hand, always begins in dryness and struggle, but ultimately brings us to a place of true freedom where there is effortless joy and pleasure with dignity.

PRAYER. *Jesus, may your truth set us free.*

S CHRISTIAN experience attests especially in prayer, the more docile we are to the promptings of grace, the more we grow in inner freedom and confidence during trials, such as those we face in the pressures and constraints of the outer world. —No. 1742

AUG. 24

REFLECTION. The only true freedom comes from obedience inspired by humility. Anyone who has tried it knows that this Zen-like contradiction is true. Conversely, rebellion born of pride is the surest way to imprisonment and misery, as the devil himself has discovered.

PRAYER. *Jesus, help us to imitate your example of humble obedience.*

***MORALLY good* act requires the goodness of the object, of the end, and of the circumstances together.** —No. 1755

AUG. 25

REFLECTION. An act is judged by what it is, why we do it, and what the result is. All three of these things need to be deemed good and worthwhile. Most of our poor moral judgments come from us settling for getting one or two of the criteria right, e.g., thinking that we can get away with a good act even if it has a bad outcome (or vice versa).

PRAYER. *Father, give us the mind of Christ.*

THERE are some concrete acts—such as fornication—that it is always wrong to choose, because choosing them entails a disorder of the will, that is, a moral evil. —No. 1755

AUG. 26

REFLECTION. As we consider an act, the circumstances, and the outcome, nothing comes easier to a human being than to find a rationalization to permit something we know is evil. Our desires want us to fool ourselves. The greater the pleasure to be gained from an act, the less we can trust our initial judgment.

PRAYER. *Lord, give us spiritual insight and free us from the illusion of desire.*

IN themselves passions are neither good nor evil. They are morally qualified only to the extent that they effectively engage reason and will. —No. 1767

AUG. 27

REFLECTION. Our passions are the drivers which push us forward to engage the world. We must count on our reason and willpower to steer a sure and certain course. To that end, we must work hard forming our intellect and strengthening our willpower.

PRAYER. *Lord, help us to purify our passions to serve the true and good.*

ORAL perfection consists in man's being moved to the good not by his will alone, but also by his sensitive appetite, as in the words of the psalm: "My heart and flesh sing for joy to the living God."†

—No. 1770

AUG. 28

REFLECTION. It is easy to imagine our spirit longing for God, but the *Catechism* suggests that even our body cries out for God. The fullness of the Christian experience is not confined to our spirits alone, but is a material, bodily experience as well.

PRAYER. *Jesus, help us to make our bodies pleasing to you.*

T IS important for every person to be sufficiently present to himself in order to hear and follow the voice of his conscience. This requirement of *interiority* is all the more necessary as life often distracts us from any reflection, self-examination or introspection. **—No. 1779**

AUG. 29

REFLECTION. The ability to "be present to ourselves" is especially difficult in today's society. True silence is rare, and solitude is usually avoided, and yet the saints have always held up solitude and silence as the surest paths to union with God.

PRAYER. *Jesus, lead us to know our true selves.*

† Ps 84:2.

HUMAN being must always obey the certain judgment of his conscience. If he were deliberately to act against it, he would condemn himself. Yet it can happen that moral conscience remains in ignorance and makes erroneous judgments about acts to be performed or already committed. —No. 1790

AUG. 30

REFLECTION. The Church insists that we must follow our conscience but it never says that our conscience is always right. Without a mastery of our will and cultivation of our reason and intellect, the judgment of our conscience can be wrong.

PRAYER. *Holy Spirit, help us to know the truth.*

GNORANCE of Christ and his Gospel, bad example given by others, enslavement to one's passions . . . rejection of the Church's authority and her teaching, lack of conversion and of charity: these can be at the source of errors of judgment in moral conduct. —No. 1792

AUG. 31

REFLECTION. Each moral issue we face in our lives is like a crossroads. The choice we make at that moment has serious consequences immediately and for the rest of our future. Let us never underestimate the importance of our choices and decisions.

PRAYER. *Jesus, strengthen us in moral courage.*

SEPT. 1

A VIRTUE is an habitual and firm disposition to do the good. It allows the person not only to perform good acts, but to give the best of himself. The virtuous person tends toward the good with all his sensory and spiritual powers; he pursues the good and chooses it in concrete actions.

—No. 1803

REFLECTION. The virtuous are in the habit of choosing correctly, until one day it is just natural for them to do the right thing. For the virtuous person, doing good is the default setting.

PRAYER. *Holy Spirit, set our hearts on fire with a love of holy wisdom.*

SEPT. 2

FOUR virtues play a pivotal role and accordingly are called "cardinal"; all the others are grouped around them. They are: prudence, justice, fortitude, and temperance.

—No. 1805

REFLECTION. The ancient philosophers who lived long before Christ articulated four commands for those who wanted to live a virtuous (i.e., strong) life: be wise, be fair, be brave, be self-controlled. The Church has always confirmed the wisdom of these counsels.

PRAYER. *Spirit of God, strengthen us to live the cardinal virtues.*

ITH the help of [prudence] we apply moral principles to particular cases without error and overcome doubts about the good to achieve and the evil to avoid. **SEPT. 3**

—No. 1806

REFLECTION. Prudence is the ability to make the right moral decision. It is an ability formed over time through careful cultivation, reading the right books, especially the Bible, paying attention to other people's stories, weighing the results of each decision and learning from your mistakes. It is hard to overstate the importance of pudence.

PRAYER. *Spirit of Wisdom and Truth, be with us, always at work in your Church.*

***USTICE* is the moral virtue that consists in the constant and firm will to give their due to God and neighbor.** **SEPT. 4**

—No. 1807

REFLECTION. Each and every single person with whom we come in contact has a special dignity as a creature made in the image of God. All of creation, too, shares in that dignity. For this reason, all creatures and all creation are "due" certain things from us, things like respect, love, aid, and depending on our relationship to them, obedience, care, protection, etc.

PRAYER. *Lord, strengthen the just and surround them with your favor.*

ORTITUDE **is the moral virtue that ensures firmness in difficulties and constancy in the pursuit of the good. It strengthens the resolve to resist temptations and to overcome obstacles in the moral life.**

SEPT. 5

—No. 1808

REFLECTION. All four of the cardinal virtues are interdependent. Prudence informs a sense of justice, and fortitude gives one the strength to persist in doing what is right. Knowing what to do is not enough—one must be strong enough to pull it off consistently, over time, habitually.

PRAYER. *Lord, strengthen our hearts to choose the right with courage.*

EMPERANCE **. . . ensures the will's mastery over instincts and keeps desires within the limits of what is honorable. The temperate person directs the sensitive appetites toward what is good and maintains a healthy discretion.**

SEPT. 6

—No. 1809

REFLECTION. The ancients spoke of "leisure with dignity," acknowledging the difficulty inherent in the human experience of fulfilling our desires without being controlled by them. Temperance controls and directs our freedom so that we can reach our full potential.

PRAYER. *Lord, strengthen us until we are stronger even than our own desires.*

FAITH is the theological virtue by which we believe in God and believe all that he has said and revealed to us, and that Holy Church proposes for our belief, because he is truth itself. —No. 1814

SEPT. 7

REFLECTION. The cardinal virtues are means to the holy life, but the theological virtues of faith, hope, and charity (i.e., love) are the ends at which they aim. The end we call faith is a life that fully embraces the truth, some of which we grasp now, and some of which we know we must live into over time.

PRAYER. *Lord, increase our faith!*

THE virtue of hope responds to the aspiration to happiness which God has placed in the heart of every man; it takes up the hopes that inspire men's activities and purifies them so as to order them to the Kingdom of heaven. —No. 1818

SEPT. 8

REFLECTION. Hope is the confident expectation that we will receive God's blessings in this life and stand in his presence in the next. Our faith tells us that there is nothing better to hope for than this. To spend eternity with God is the end of all our Christian practices.

PRAYER. *Lord, increase our desire for heaven.*

HARITY is the theological virtue by which we love God above all things for his own sake, and our neighbor as ourselves for the love of God. —No. 1822

SEPT. 9

REFLECTION. It was St. Paul who first articulated the theological virtues of faith, hope, and love,† and he was quick to point out that love is the greatest of the three. This highest of all virtues Paul described as angelic patience, a kindness without exception, a genuine humility, and a firm belief in the goodness of all people and things.

PRAYER. *Lord, help us to live in love always.*

HE practice of all the virtues is animated and inspired by charity, which "binds everything together in perfect harmony"††; it is the *form of the virtues* . . . it is the source and the goal of their Christian practice. —No. 1827

SEPT. 10

REFLECTION. His emphasis on love is what separates Paul from the ancient philosophers and the Greco-Roman mythology that surrounded him. Paul insisted that self-giving love—in imitation of Christ—is the distinguishing feature of Christianity. Without it, all other Christian practices are worthless.

PRAYER. *Lord, help us to give love its proper place in our lives.*

† Cf. 1 Cor 13.
†† Col 3:14.

IN is an offense against God. . . . Like the first sin, it is disobedience, a revolt against God through the will to become "like gods,"† knowing and determining good and evil. —No. 1850

SEPT. 11

REFLECTION. When Adam and Eve ate from "the tree of Good and Evil," they thought they would gain an intellectual knowledge of good and evil and in that way be like God, but unfortunately, all they gained was experiential knowledge of good and evil. Experience is a hard teacher, and the experience of evil is the hardest and cruelest of all lessons.

PRAYER. *Lord, teach us to obey you with childlike trust.*

ORTAL sin **destroys charity in the heart of man by a grave violation of God's law; it turns man away from God, who is his ultimate end and his beatitude, by preferring an inferior good to him.**

Venial sin **allows charity to subsist, even though it offends and wounds it.** —No. 1855

SEPT. 12

REFLECTION. Every sin is a choice to settle for less than we really want or deserve. It takes reflection and cultivation to overcome our attraction to novelty and our evil impulses in order to choose what is truly good.

PRAYER. *Guide us in your truth, O God.*

† Gen 3:5.

SEPT. 13

VENIAL sin weakens charity; it manifests a disordered affection for created goods; it impedes the soul's progress in the exercise of the virtues and the practice of the moral good; it merits temporal punishment.

—No. 1863

REFLECTION. We should always prefer God to the things he has created. But as we drift away from God, we become more and more self-centered and our desires slide lower and lower on the scale until mere things become more important to us than even the people we love.

PRAYER. *Father, help us to prefer you over everything else.*

SEPT. 14

SIN creates a proclivity to sin; it engenders vice by repetition of the same acts. This results in perverse inclinations which cloud conscience and corrupt the concrete judgment of good and evil. Thus sin tends to reproduce itself and reinforce itself, but it cannot destroy the moral sense at its root.

—No. 1865

REFLECTION. Just as virtue is habitual, so sin becomes a default setting for those who are not vigilant enough to guard against it. It is easy to go downhill, and few things are easier than to sink slowly, imperceptibly into vice and addiction.

PRAYER. *Lord, save us from our own evil inclinations.*

SEPT. 15

HE human person needs to live in society. Society is not for him an extraneous addition but a requirement of his nature. Through the exchange with others, mutual service and dialogue with his brethren, man develops his potential. . . .† —No. 1879

REFLECTION. Two attitudes toward society are common. Either we feel inferior and are intimidated, or we feel superior and can't be bothered. In fact, both are true! In some ways we are weaker than others, and in some ways stronger—through social engagement the human family completes each other.

PRAYER. *Lord, help us to love our neighbor as ourselves.*

SEPT. 16

O PROMOTE the participation of the greatest number in the life of a society, the creation of voluntary associations and institutions must be encouraged "on both national and international levels, which relate to economic and social goals, to cultural and recreational activities, to sport, to various professions, and to political affairs."†† —No. 1882

REFLECTION. Just as animals gather in herds or flocks, so human beings are meant to form groups. Whether it is softball leagues or the museum society, human beings are meant to be joiners.

PRAYER. *Lord, strengthen the bonds of the body of Christ.*

† Cf. GS 25 § 1.
†† John XXIII, *MM* 60.

OD has not willed to reserve to himself all exercise of power. He entrusts to every creature the functions it is capable of performing, according to the capacities of its own nature. —No. 1884

SEPT. 17

REFLECTION. God trusts his creatures to govern themselves, and all leaders should govern in a way that allows those in their charge to exercise freedom and choose what is good. But just as God provides guidelines and support for that endeavor, so should those who lead and govern.

PRAYER. *Father, give us wise and honest leaders.*

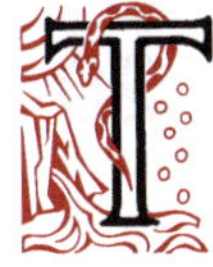

HE duty of obedience requires all to give due honor to authority and to treat those who are charged to exercise it with respect, and, insofar as it is deserved, with gratitude and good-will. —No. 1900

SEPT. 18

REFLECTION. It is natural for people to complain about those who lead them, to resist their efforts, and to undermine their authority, but, except for rare cases, it is not proper to our faith, and can be quite harmful to the greater good.

PRAYER. *Lord, teach us to support and pray for our leaders.*

UTHORITY is exercised legitimately only when it seeks the common good of the group concerned and if it employs morally licit means to attain it. If rulers were to enact unjust laws or take measures contrary to the moral order, such arrangements would not be binding in conscience. —No. 1903

SEPT. 19

REFLECTION. Although the *Catechism*, following the Bible, directs Christians to be obedient to those in authority, it is careful to point out that one need not remain under an unjust authority.

PRAYER. *Lord, inspire leaders to desire the good for those in their charge.*

"

ARTICIPATION" is the voluntary and generous engagement of a person in social interchange. It is necessary that all participate, each according to his position and role, in promoting the common good. This obligation is inherent in the dignity of the human person. —No. 1913

SEPT. 20

REFLECTION. The defeatist attitude that creates a frustrated citizen with no desire to participate in the social order is not the Christian way. It is the duty of a social being to influence society, especially by living an ordered and honest life of service to others.

PRAYER. *Lord, help us to truly be salt for the earth.*

THE differences among persons belong to God's plan, who wills that we should need one another. These differences should encourage charity.

—No. 1946

SEPT. 21

REFLECTION. The jigsaw puzzle is a wonderful example of God's intention for humanity. It is only because all of the shapes are different that they fit together tightly. The more pieces that come together, the clearer the picture is. There is a feeling of incompleteness when even just one piece is missing.

PRAYER. *Father, unite all your people wherever they may be.*

THE natural law is a participation in God's wisdom and goodness by man formed in the image of his Creator. It expresses the dignity of the human person and forms the basis of his fundamental rights and duties. —No. 1978

SEPT. 22

REFLECTION. Being in God's image we have an innate sense of right and wrong which does not change from time to time or person to person but is fundamental to beings made in God's image, for it is based upon the nature of who God is.

PRAYER. *Father, open our eyes to see the wonders of your law.*

THE Law of Moses contains many truths naturally accessible to reason. God has revealed them because men did not read them in their hearts. —No. 1981

SEPT. 23

REFLECTION. God has to make explicit in the Bible and Revelation what is implicit in our nature because we aren't paying attention to what he has written in our hearts. This is why God had to drive his people into the desert, so that he could get their attention.

PRAYER. *Lord, soften our hearts that we may hear your voice.*

THE Law of the Gospel fulfills and surpasses the Old Law and brings it to perfection. . . .

The New Law is a law of love, a law of grace, a law of freedom.

—Nos. 1984-1985

SEPT. 24

REFLECTION. Although the New Testament can be read and understood on its own, it reveals its truest power when read in light of the God of the Old Testament who loves his people by giving them laws and leaders. Jesus takes it to the next level of love, grace, and freedom.

PRAYER. *Jesus, tune our minds to hear you and keep your words.*

SEPT. 25

USTIFICATION has been merited for us by the Passion of Christ. It is granted us through Baptism. It conforms us to the righteousness of God, who justifies us. . . . It is the most excellent work of God's mercy. —No. 2020

REFLECTION. As human beings, we are not afraid to ask if someone's actions are justified. In this way, we discuss whether or not the action is the right one for the situation. When God sent his Son to die for us, he said to the universe, these humans are worth the effort.

PRAYER. *Lord, help us to grasp the dignity of every human being.*

SEPT. 26

HE divine initiative in the work of grace precedes, prepares, and elicits the free response of man. Grace responds to the deepest yearnings of human freedom, calls freedom to cooperate with it, and perfects freedom. —No. 2022

REFLECTION. God's grace is so abundant and so pervasive, that, like oxygen, we rarely grasp how important it is. But when things fall apart and everything looks dark, we cry out to God almost as a reflex. In those moments, we realize that our lives are totally in God's hands.

PRAYER. *Father, keep us always in your grace.*

E CAN have merit in God's sight only because of God's free plan to associate man with the work of his grace. Merit is to be ascribed in the first place to the grace of God, and secondly to man's collaboration. Man's merit is due to God.

—No. 2025

SEPT. 27

REFLECTION. God is like a parent playing checkers with his five-year-old. He wants to let the child win, but the child has to make the right moves. That tiny bit of cooperation is our merit, and even that is due to God's willing it.

PRAYER. *Lord, accept our efforts to cooperate with your grace.*

T IS in the Church, in communion with all the baptized, that the Christian fulfills his vocation. From the Church he receives the Word of God. . . . From the Church he receives the grace of the sacraments. . . . From the Church he learns the *example of holiness* . . . he discovers it in the spiritual tradition and long history of the saints. **—No. 2030**

SEPT. 28

REFLECTION. You can't be a Christian alone; and God calls no one to an exclusive one-on-one relationship with him. To be a Christian you must belong to and participate in the Church.

PRAYER. *Father, teach us to love the Church.*

ROM generation to generation, under the aegis and vigilance of the pastors, the "deposit" of Christian moral teaching has been handed on, a deposit composed of a characteristic body of rules, commandments, and virtues proceeding from faith in Christ and animated by charity.

—No. 2033

SEPT. 29

REFLECTION. We can't figure this all out on our own in the small amount of time we've been given—we're not supposed to. That's why the Church preserves the wisdom of the saints and the teachings of the Bible for each generation to learn from and to add to it.

PRAYER. *Lord, raise up teachers for your Church.*

N HER motherly care, the Church grants us the mercy of God. . . . With a mother's foresight she also lavishes on us day after day in her liturgy the nourishment of the Word and Eucharist of our Lord. —No. 2040

SEPT. 30

REFLECTION. Just as we have times of disagreement and times when we feel closer to or farther from our own parents, so our relationship with the Church may wax and wane, but it can never be severed. She will always be our mother.

PRAYER. *Father, draw all people into the arms of the Church.*

THE precepts of the Church are set in the context of a moral life bound to and nourished by liturgical life. The obligatory character of these positive laws decreed by the pastoral authorities is meant to guarantee to the faithful the very necessary minimum in the spirit of prayer and moral effort, in the growth in love of God and neighbor.

—No. 2041

OCT. 1

REFLECTION. In order to help its members live a holy and moral life the church has set up "minimum requirements" to be observed by all who consider themselves Catholic.

PRAYER. *Lord, make your Church one in mind and heart.*

THE first precept ("You shall attend Mass on Sundays and on holy days of obligation and rest from servile labor") requires the faithful to sanctify the day commemorating the Resurrection of the Lord as well as the principal liturgical feasts honoring the mysteries of the Lord, the Blessed Virgin Mary, and the saints. . . .† —No. 2042

OCT. 2

REFLECTION. The first precept underscores the communal nature of the Church—when everyone is gathered you need to be there—and it also highlights our need to sanctify time, giving at least one day a week to God.

PRAYER. *Father, accept the worship of your Church at prayer.*

† Cf. CIC, cann. 1246-1248; CCEO, can. 880 § 3, 881 §§ 1, 2, 4.

HE second precept ("You shall confess your sins at least once a year") ensures preparation for the Eucharist by the reception of the sacrament of reconciliation, which continues Baptism's work of conversion and forgiveness.†

—No. 2042

OCT. 3

REFLECTION. If one is going to be required to receive communion once a year (third precept), it is important that one prepare for it by going to confession beforehand. It follows that if one receives communion more frequently than once a year one ought to go to confession more often. Once a month is usually recommended.

PRAYER. *Lord, draw us more often to receive the sacraments of our salvation.*

HE third precept ("You shall receive the sacrament of the Eucharist at least during the Easter season") guarantees as a minimum the reception of the Lord's Body and Blood in connection with the Paschal feasts, the origin and center of the Christian liturgy.†† —No. 2042

OCT. 4

REFLECTION. Notice how the Church separates the reception of communion (at least once a year) from attending Mass (every week). Two points follow: first, we must be prepared to receive communion, and even if we aren't, we still need to gather with the Church.

PRAYER. *Lord Jesus, sanctify your Church by the gift of the Eucharist.*

† Cf. CIC, can. 989; CCEO, can. 719.

†† Cf. CIC, can. 920; CCEO, cann. 708; 881 § 3.

THE fourth precept ("You shall observe the days of fasting and abstinence established by the Church") ensures the times of ascesis and penance which prepare us for the liturgical feasts and help us acquire mastery over our instincts and freedom of heart.† —No. 2043

OCT. 5

REFLECTION. The fourth precept also underscores the importance of the Easter season and that we ought to prepare for it. The return of the Lenten fast is a yearly examination of our life and a chance to improve ourselves to better serve the risen Christ.

PRAYER. *Lord of the desert, help us to make use of the season of Lent.*

THE fifth precept ("You shall help to provide for the needs of the Church") means that the faithful are obliged to assist with the material needs of the Church, each according to his own ability.†† —No. 2043

OCT. 6

REFLECTION. As more and more lay people take roles in the Church, there is less free labor in the form of priests and sisters to serve the people of God. This makes it more important than ever that parishioners support their parish "according to their ability."

PRAYER. *Father, make me a cheerful giver to the work of the Church.*

† Cf. CIC, cann. 1249-1251; CCEO, can. 882.

†† Cf. CIC, can. 222; CCEO, can. 25. *Furthermore, episcopal conferences can establish other ecclesiastical precepts for their own territories* (Cf. CIC, can. 455).

IN ORDER that the message of salvation can show the power of its truth and radiance before men, it must be authenticated by the witness of the life of Christians. —No. 2044

OCT. 7

REFLECTION. Christians spend a lot of time and money on their faith, but if it doesn't make a tangible and visible difference in their lives, especially during difficult times, what's the point of being a Christian? Christianity should make a visible, measurable difference in our lives.

PRAYER. *Lord Jesus, be real to me, and help me be authentic in my relationship with you.*

THE gift of the Commandments is the gift of God himself and his holy will. In making his will known, God reveals himself to his people. —No. 2059

OCT. 8

REFLECTION. The Ten Commandments tell us a lot about God, but at the bottom of it all is the clear fact that God cares for us. Any parent knows that setting commands and boundaries for your kids is a sign of love.

PRAYER. *Lord, may our love show in our obedience to you.*

HE Ten Commandments state what is required in the love of God and love of neighbor. The first three concern love of God, and the other seven love of neighbor. —No. 2067

OCT. 9

REFLECTION. The Ten Commandments are concrete "actionable" ways in which we can serve God here on earth. When one considers that only three of the ten Commandments are focused on God, we understand that serving God is most evident in the way we treat others.

PRAYER. *Father, help us to see Christ in others.*

HE Decalogue forms a coherent whole. . . . To transgress one commandment is to infringe all the others.† . . . The Decalogue brings man's religious and social life into unity. —No. 2069

OCT. 10

REFLECTION. To the young and immature, rules are meant to be picked apart and manipulated through dissection and hairsplitting. In the moral life, it is only through practice of the commandments, in humility and obedience, that the beauty and power of the whole moral law is revealed.

PRAYER. *Christ, help us to learn obedience in our trials and sufferings.*

† Cf. Jas 2:10-11.

INCE they express man's fundamental duties towards God and towards his neighbor, the Ten Commandments reveal, in their primordial content, *grave* obligations. They are fundamentally immutable, and they oblige always and everywhere. No one can dispense from them.

—No. 2072

OCT. 11

REFLECTION. As the *Catechism* describes them, the Ten Commandments are a big deal—requirements from which we are not lightly excused. We ought to be concerned about following them closely, but many people couldn't name half of them, and we cannot follow them if we don't know them.

PRAYER. *Lord, teach us to love your law.*

O ADORE God is to praise and exalt him and to humble oneself. . . . The worship of the one God sets man free from turning in on himself, from the slavery of sin and the idolatry of the world. —No. 2097

OCT. 12

REFLECTION. The first commandment gets man going in the right direction—outward, away from himself and his false idols, and upward, beyond this life toward his sublime and transcendent destiny.

PRAYER. *God, help us to see you as you are.*

HE first commandment forbids honoring gods other than the one Lord who has revealed himself to his people. It proscribes superstition and irreligion. Superstition in some sense represents a perverse excess of religion; irreligion is the vice contrary by defect to the virtue of religion. —No. 2110

OCT. 13

REFLECTION. Appropriate faith in God is not easy because it means finding the middle way between two very common human mistakes—skepticism and superstition, that is, between our tendency to deny the supernatural and our lust to control it.

PRAYER. *Father, help us to worship you in spirit and truth.*

MONG all the words of Revelation, there is one which is unique: the revealed name of God. God confides his name to those who believe in him. . . . The gift of a name belongs to the order of trust and intimacy. —No. 2143

OCT. 14

REFLECTION. The second commandment reflects a respect for the power of words and especially for people's names that is hard to recapture in our day, but by obeying this commandment and giving God this respect we learn to give it to others as well.

PRAYER. *Lord, may every knee bend at the sound of your name.*

OCT. 15

EVERYONE'S name is sacred. The name is the icon of the person. . . .

The name one receives is a name for eternity. In the kingdom, the mysterious and unique character of each person marked with God's name will shine forth in splendor. —Nos. 2158-2159

REFLECTION. The second commandment reminds us of what the ancients believed—that a person's name is a sacred representation of that person, the use of which should not be taken lightly.

PRAYER. *Lord, you call each of us by name.*

OCT. 16

IF GOD "rested and was refreshed" on the seventh day, man too ought to "rest" and should let others, especially the poor, "be refreshed."† . . . It is a day of protest against the servitude of work and the worship of money.†† —No. 2172

REFLECTION. Periodic abstinence from the things we desire—even from the things we need—is a common practice in Christianity. Sunday gives us a chance to get and keep our priorities straight where money and work are concerned.

PRAYER. *Father, may we learn from you the rhythm of work and rest.*

† Ex 31:17; cf. 23:12.

†† Cf. Neh 13:15-22; 2 Chr 36:21.

HE fourth commandment opens the second table of the Decalogue. It shows us the order of charity. God has willed that, after him, we should honor our parents to whom we owe life and who have handed on to us the knowledge of God. —No. 2197

OCT. 17

REFLECTION. Our parents have a unique place in terms of important relationships in our lives. The parallels between our relationship with God and the relationship of a parent and a child are important reflections for those seeking to understand the ways of God.

PRAYER. *Father of Love, teach us to love our families as you love us.*

N THE Sermon on the Mount, the Lord recalls the commandment, "You shall not kill,"† and adds to it the proscription of anger, hatred, and vengeance. Going further, Christ asks his disciples to turn the other cheek, to love their enemies.†† —No. 2262

OCT. 18

REFLECTION. The fifth commandment forbidding murder stands in the middle of the Decalogue underscoring the basic message of all the commandments: God has created life and we are to support and respect that life and do nothing to diminish or destroy it.

PRAYER. *Lord, teach us the real value of a human life.*

† Mt 5:21.
†† Cf. Mt 5:22-39; 5:44.

EVERYONE is responsible for his life before God who has given it to him. It is God who remains the sovereign Master of life. . . . We are stewards, not owners, of the life God has entrusted to us. It is not ours to dispose of. —No. 2280

OCT. 19

REFLECTION. The fifth commandment forbids suicide and other self-destructive and risky behavior. A culture that does not respect all forms of life will soon be a culture in which no life is sacred, even one's own.

PRAYER. *Lord, help us to form a culture of life in our world.*

SEXUALITY, in which man's belonging to the bodily and biological world is expressed, becomes personal and truly human when it is integrated into the relationship of one person to another, in the complete and lifelong mutual gift of a man and a woman. —No. 2337

OCT. 20

REFLECTION. The sixth commandment ("You shall not commit adultery") protects the divine image in man, for to have sexual relations outside of marriage, that is, apart from a lifelong, exclusive relationship of one man and one woman, is an act that is offensive to the dignity of marriage and a grave sin.

PRAYER. *Father, teach us how to honor our bodies.*

HASTITY includes an *apprenticeship of self-mastery* which is a training in human freedom. The alternative is clear: either man governs his passions and finds peace, or he lets himself be dominated by them and becomes unhappy.† —No. 2339

OCT. 21

REFLECTION. The secular notion of freedom demands the right to completely indulge without guilt or inhibition, whereas Christianity has always insisted that man can only find true freedom in self-mastery where he is always in control and can enjoy without regret.

PRAYER. *Lord, help us to rule over our own will and desires.*

HE seventh commandment forbids unjustly taking or keeping the goods of one's neighbor and wronging him in any way with respect to his goods. . . . Christian life strives to order this world's goods to God and to fraternal charity. —No. 2401

OCT. 22

REFLECTION. If we strive to order our lives and all this world's goods toward God and our neighbor we will have no problem obeying the commandments. Or, put another way, if we obey these commandments we will have no problem ordering our lives to God and our neighbor. Obedience is essential to the well-ordered life.

PRAYER. *Lord, teach us to obey.*

† Cf. Sir 1:22.

HE eighth commandment forbids misrepresenting the truth in our relations with others. This moral prescription flows from the vocation of the holy people to bear witness to their God who is the truth and wills the truth.

—No. 2464

OCT. 23

REFLECTION. The commandments reveal the nature of God. God is the truth. If we want to be children of God, be like God, then we must always speak the truth and live lives of integrity.

PRAYER. *Lord, keep watch at the door of my lips.*

Y ITS very nature, lying is to be condemned. It is a profanation of speech, whereas the purpose of speech is to communicate known truth to others.

—No. 2485

OCT. 24

REFLECTION. The *Catechism* suggests that the whole point of speech organs is to pass on the truth to others. This does not rule out humor, song, or story, for the best of these contain deep and abiding truths.

PRAYER. *Lord, may we always speak the truth in love.*

TRUTH in words . . . is necessary to man, who is endowed with intellect. But truth can also find other complementary forms of human expression, above all when it is a matter of evoking what is beyond words: the depths of the human heart, the exaltations of the soul, the mystery of God. —No. 2500

OCT. 25

REFLECTION. Art is true when it reflects the dignity of man's divine nature and when it reveals to men the beauty and splendor of truth.

PRAYER. *Father, inspire artists to reveal to us in their work visions of your glorious truth.*

BECAUSE man is a *composite being, spirit and body,* there already exists a certain tension in him; a certain struggle of tendencies between "spirit" and "flesh" develops. . . . It is part of the daily experience of the spiritual battle. —No. 2516

OCT. 26

REFLECTION. The ninth commandment urges us to keep our physical desires in harmony with our spiritual dignity. To do so requires a daily battle against the desires to possess, control, and consume.

PRAYER. *Father, help us to honor your Spirit within us.*

URITY of heart is the precondition of the vision of God. Even now it enables us to see *according to* God . . . ; it lets us perceive the human body—ours and our neighbor's—as a temple of the Holy Spirit, a manifestation of divine beauty. —No. 2519

OCT. 27

REFLECTION. Much of our moral life is interior. Our minds can go wrong long before our actions do. Purity begins with our thoughts, and then depends on our eyes: what we choose to look at and why.

PRAYER. *Lord, inspire our vision that we may see as you do.*

HE tenth commandment forbids *greed* and the desire to amass earthly goods without limit. It forbids *avarice* arising from a passion for riches and their attendant power. —No. 2536

OCT. 28

REFLECTION. When the child heaps food upon his plate and only eats a little bit he is told, "Your eyes are bigger than your stomach." In the same way our desire to possess is much greater than what we actually need to be satisfied.

PRAYER. *Jesus, help us be content with a little.*

OCT. 29

ENVY is a capital sin. It refers to the sadness at the sight of another's goods and the immoderate desire to acquire them for oneself, even unjustly. When it wishes grave harm to a neighbor it is a mortal sin: . . . —No. 2539

REFLECTION. The three primary drives that we must battle daily are the desires to possess, control, and consume. The best weapon against these drives is a grateful heart and a humble spirit.

PRAYER. *Lord, free us from the slavery of envy and covetousness.*

OCT. 30

JESUS enjoins his disciples to prefer him to everything and everyone, and bids them "renounce all that [they have]" for his sake and that of the Gospel.† . . . The precept of detachment from riches is obligatory for entrance into the Kingdom of heaven. —No. 2544

REFLECTION. It is not how much we have that matters, but how attached we are to it. There is no sin in being rich if you are not controlled by your possessions. Likewise, there is no virtue in being poor if you don't love God above all things.

PRAYER. *Father, teach us to love you above all things.*

† Lk 14:33; cf. Mk 8:35.

ESIRE for true happiness frees man from his immoderate attachment to the goods of this world so that he can find his fulfillment in the vision and beatitude of God. —No. 2548

OCT. 31

REFLECTION. Once you taste the true joy of the spiritual life and compare it with the passing happiness of transitory things, the commandments aren't as difficult. Lying, cheating, stealing, and adultery seem like an awful lot of trouble for anything less than true happiness.

PRAYER. *Jesus, teach us to desire true happiness.*

"RAYER is the raising of one's mind and heart to God or the requesting of good things from God."† But when we pray, do we speak from the height of our pride and will, or "out of the depths" of a humble and contrite heart?†† He who humbles himself will be exalted;††† *humility* is the foundation of prayer. —No. 2559

NOV. 1

REFLECTION. People have different ideas about the purpose and method of prayer, but none can deny that prayer begins by admitting our own limitations and our need for God.

PRAYER. *Lord, soften my heart and shape it for you.*

† St. John Damascene, *De fide orth.* 3, 24: PG 94, 1089C.
†† Ps 130:1.
††† Cf. Lk 18:9-14.

THE wonder of prayer is revealed beside the well where we come seeking water: there, Christ comes to meet every human being. It is he who first seeks us and asks us for a drink. Jesus thirsts; his asking arises from the depths of God's desire for us. Whether we realize it or not, prayer is the encounter of God's thirst with ours. —No. 2560

NOV. 2

REFLECTION. As the *Catechism* nears its end we are brought back to the point made by the very first number of the *Catechism*—that God is seeking us.

PRAYER. *Lord, may our hearts respond to the sound of your voice.*

IN NAMING the source of prayer, Scripture speaks sometimes of the soul or the spirit, but most often of the heart (more than a thousand times). According to Scripture, it is the *heart* that prays. If our heart is far from God, the words of prayer are in vain. —No. 2562

NOV. 3

REFLECTION. Whether in ancient Biblical languages or in modern English, the concept of "the heart" represents the deepest, truest part of a human being. It is that part of us, our heart, which we must give to God in prayer.

PRAYER. *Lord, turn our hearts toward you.*

N THE New Covenant, prayer is the living relationship of the children of God with their Father who is good beyond measure, with his Son Jesus Christ and with the Holy Spirit. . . . Thus, the life of prayer is the habit of being in the presence of the thrice-holy God and in communion with him.—No. 2565

NOV. 4

REFLECTION. To get used to the company of the people we live and work with takes time. The same is true of our relationship with God. We need to pray often to become comfortable in God's company.

PRAYER. *Holy Trinity, make a home in our homes.*

HE living and true God tirelessly calls each person to that mysterious encounter known as prayer. In prayer, the faithful God's initiative of love always comes first; our own first step is always a response. As God gradually reveals himself and reveals man to himself, prayer appears as a reciprocal call, a covenant drama. —No. 2567

NOV. 5

REFLECTION. Prayer is not meant to be a one-way monologue, a daily recitation of fears, needs, and desires, but a real covenant relationship built, like all relationships, on an honest exchange of hearts.

PRAYER. *Lord, draw near to us as we seek you.*

HEN God calls him, Abraham goes forth "as the Lord had told him";† Abraham's heart is entirely submissive to the Word and so he obeys. Such attentiveness of the heart, whose decisions are made according to God's will, is essential to prayer, while the words used count only in relation to it.

—No. 2570

NOV. 6

REFLECTION. Prayer often seems focused on God's actions, but in order for prayer to be truly a two-way relationship, we must find that prayer also influences how we act and what we do.

PRAYER. *Father, let us live the prayerful thoughts of our hearts.*

BRAHAM'S first prayer in words [is] a veiled complaint reminding God of his promises which seem unfulfilled.†† Thus one aspect of the drama of prayer appears from the beginning: the test of faith in the fidelity of God.

—No. 2570

NOV. 7

REFLECTION. The harsh reality of unanswered prayer is neither a sign that we are unworthy nor proof that God does not exist; it is part of the mystery of the relationship between God and man. To give up when our prayers are not answered is to treat God like an out-of-order vending machine.

PRAYER. *Lord, hear our prayer.*

† Gen 12:4.
†† Cf. Gen 15:2f.

BEFORE confronting his elder brother Esau, Jacob wrestles all night with a mysterious figure who refuses to reveal his name, but who blesses him before leaving him at dawn. From this account, the spiritual tradition of the Church has retained the symbol of prayer as a battle of faith and as the triumph of perseverance.† —No. 2573

NOV. 8

REFLECTION. There is a struggle in prayer, as in any healthy relationship. God does not answer every request with an immediate "Yes, sir." What full partner in a relationship of love would do so?

PRAYER. *Lord, grant us perseverance in prayer.*

THE arguments of [Moses'] prayer . . . will inspire the boldness of the great intercessors among the Jewish people and in the Church: God is love; he is therefore righteous and faithful; he cannot contradict himself; he must remember his marvellous deeds, since his glory is at stake, and he cannot forsake this people that bears his name. —No. 2577

NOV. 9

REFLECTION. Moses' intercession starts with God, not with the people he is interceding for. Moses urges God to intercede not primarily for the people's sake, but for God's sake, the sake of his name and holiness.

PRAYER. *Lord, remember your love for your people.*

† Cf. Gen 32:24-30; Lk 18:1-8.

IN THE Psalms David, inspired by the Holy Spirit, is the first prophet of Jewish and Christian prayer. The prayer of Christ, the true Messiah and Son of David, will reveal and fulfill the meaning of this prayer.

—No. 2579

NOV. 10

REFLECTION. The book of Psalms is one of the most important books of the Bible. In it, we learn from God's chosen people how we are to address him. The power of the psalms rests upon the fact that they record people of prayer engaging God with every possible human emotion.

PRAYER. *Father, hear us whenever we call upon you.*

THE Psalter is the book in which The Word of God becomes man's prayer. . . . In him [Christ], the psalms continue to teach us how to pray.

—No. 2587

NOV. 11

REFLECTION. The psalms have been prayed daily since before the time of Jesus. In the Christian tradition the psalms are prayed by priests, nuns, and monks, and lay people, daily in the Liturgy of the Hours. It has been said that one who does not have an intimate familiarity with the psalms does not really know the fullness of prayer.

PRAYER. *Jesus, teach us how to pray.*

THE drama of prayer is fully revealed to us in the Word who became flesh and dwells among us. —No. 2598

NOV. 12

REFLECTION. Jesus is the ultimate model for our lives. Although Jesus is God, it is in his humanity that he models the life of prayer. He shows us that even he has a real need for relationship with his heavenly Father; he prays often, struggles in prayer, and teaches his disciples how to pray.

PRAYER. *Word of God, inspire our prayers.*

JESUS prays *before* the decisive moments of his mission: before his Father's witness to him during his baptism and Transfiguration, and before his own fulfillment of the Father's plan of love by his Passion.† —No. 2600

NOV. 13

REFLECTION. The idea of beginning any undertaking with a prayer to our divine creator is deep in the race. We see it in Plato, Virgil, Shakespeare, Bach, and, of course, Christ himself modeled this pattern for us.

PRAYER. *Lord, may all that we do begin in you, and in you find its completion.*

† Cf. Lk 3:21; 9:28; 22:41-44.

JESUS' prayer, characterized by thanksgiving, reveals to us how to ask: *before* the gift is given, Jesus commits himself to the One who in giving gives himself. The Giver is more precious than the gift; he is the "treasure"; in him abides his Son's heart; the gift is given "as well."†

NOV. 14

—No. 2604

REFLECTION. We ask for many things in prayer, but the real answer to the prayer is to receive God himself, who contains within himself more than we could ever ask for or imagine.

PRAYER. *Lord, you are all we need.*

ALL the troubles, for all time, of humanity enslaved by sin and death, all the petitions and intercessions of salvation history are summed up in this cry of the incarnate Word. Here the Father accepts them and, beyond all hope, answers them by raising his Son. Thus is fulfilled and brought to completion the drama of prayer in the economy of creation and salvation.

NOV. 15

—No. 2606

REFLECTION. Jesus' final cry on the cross, and God's response raising him from the dead, is the archetype played out in every true relationship of prayer.

PRAYER. *Father, hear our prayers as you heard the cry of your Son.*

† Mt 6:21, 33.

NOV. 16

ROM the *Sermon on the Mount* onwards, Jesus insists on *conversion of heart:* reconciliation with one's brother before presenting an offering on the altar, love of enemies, and prayer for persecutors, prayer to the Father in secret, not heaping up empty phrases, prayerful forgiveness from the depths of the heart, purity of heart, and seeking the Kingdom before all else.† —No. 2608

REFLECTION. Just as coherent speech and writing comes from a well-ordered thought process, so a good prayer comes from a pure heart in a right relationship to God and neighbor.

PRAYER. *Father, be patient with our efforts at prayer.*

NOV. 17

NCE committed to conversion, the heart learns to pray in *faith.* Faith is a filial adherence to God beyond what we feel and understand. It is possible because the beloved Son gives us access to the Father. —No. 2609

REFLECTION. The *Catechism,* following Scripture and Tradition, sees the parent-child relationship as illuminating our relationship with God. The sacrificial love of a parent inspires the childlike faith that binds parent and child together.

PRAYER. *Father, remember your children as we cry out to you.*

† Cf. Mt 5:23-24, 44-45; 6:7, 14-15, 21, 25, 33.

"HATEVER you ask in prayer, believe that you receive it, and you will."† Such is the power of prayer and of faith that does not doubt: "all things are possible to him who believes."†† —No. 2610

NOV. 18

REFLECTION. Faith is the key that unlocks the door to all our truest desires; but faith is not just praying with more strength or willpower. Mountain-moving faith is the result of a long and loving relationship with our God, to the point of sharing in the trust that exists between the Father and the Son.

PRAYER. *Lord Jesus, increase our faith!*

[ESUS] calls his hearers to conversion and faith, but also to *watchfulness*. . . . In communion with their Master, the disciples' prayer is a battle; only by keeping watch in prayer can one avoid falling into temptation.††† —No. 2612

NOV. 19

REFLECTION. Prayer would be important if it were only about getting our needs met, but there is an element of peril and danger about our life on earth which is also addressed in prayer. The many threats that surround our bodies and souls should lead us to the watchful attitude Jesus urged us to have.

PRAYER. *Lord, help us to remain awake with you.*

† Mk 11:24.
†† Mk 9:23; cf. Mt 21:22.
††† Cf. Lk 22:40, 46.

NOV. 20

HE urgent request of the blind men, "Have mercy on us, Son of David" or "Jesus, Son of David, have mercy on me!" has been renewed in the traditional prayer to Jesus known as the *Jesus Prayer:* "Lord Jesus Christ, Son of God, have mercy on me, a sinner!"†

—No. 2616

REFLECTION. In the Orthodox and Eastern rite traditions, the Jesus prayer is recited over and over again until it becomes a permanent tape loop in one's mind. How much more beneficial than having an annoying song or commercial jingle in our head!

PRAYER. *Lord Jesus Christ, Son of God, have mercy on me, a sinner.*

NOV. 21

HE Gospel reveals to us how Mary prays and intercedes in faith. At Cana,†† the mother of Jesus asks her son for the needs of a wedding feast; this is the sign of another feast—that of the wedding of the Lamb where he gives his body and blood at the request of the Church, his Bride. —No. 2618

REFLECTION. In the wedding at Cana, Scripture shows us both Mary's intercessory power with her son and her ultimate message to those serving Christ, "Do whatever he tells you."

PRAYER. *Mary, pray to your Son for us.*

† Mt 9:27; Mk 10:48.

†† Cf. Jn 2:1-12.

THE prayers of the Virgin Mary, in her Fiat and Magnificat, are characterized by the generous offering of her whole being in faith. —No. 2622

NOV. 22

REFLECTION. Whether in the short response of faith to Gabriel's message, "I am the handmaid of the Lord,"† or in the longer outpouring of her heart in response to the words of Elizabeth, "My soul magnifies the Lord . . . ,"†† Mary's prayers to God exemplify a heart that is completely turned over to God in love, trust, and sacrifice.

PRAYER. *Lord, help us to follow the example of your mother's love and sacrifice.*

BLESSING expresses the basic movement of Christian prayer: it is an encounter between God and man. In blessing, God's gift and man's acceptance of it are united in dialogue with each other. The prayer of blessing is man's response to God's gifts. —No. 2626

NOV. 23

REFLECTION. To bless literally means to say good things about someone. When we bless God we speak the truth about God in all his goodness, and we are in turn blessed by the action.

PRAYER. *Lord, you are good to us, and deserving of all our love.*

† Lk 1:38.
†† Lk 1:46-55.

DORATION **is the first attitude of man acknowledging that he is a creature before his Creator. . . . Adoration of the thrice-holy and sovereign God of love blends with humility and gives assurance to our supplications.**

—No. 2628

NOV. 24

REFLECTION. Adoration is an expression of the tremendous humility we feel when we truly sense God's presence. The culture idiom of "falling on your knees" expresses the humility provoked by the presence of the divine.

PRAYER. *Lord, we adore you and we pray to you.*

Y PRAYER of petition we express awareness of our relationship with God. We are creatures who are not our own beginning, not the masters of adversity, not our own last end. **—No. 2629**

NOV. 25

REFLECTION. There are those who feel that prayers of petition are somehow selfish or lacking the fullness of devotion for God that praise and adoration express, and yet, petition is an important manifestation of our own sense of right relationship to God, our need for his help, and our faith in his love for us.

PRAYER. *Lord, help us to value you above all the gifts you give us.*

T HE first movement of the prayer of petition is *asking forgiveness,* like the tax collector in the parable: "God, be merciful to me a sinner!"† It is a prerequisite for righteous and pure prayer.

—No. 2631

NOV. 26

REFLECTION. When we come to God in prayer, we do not ask for forgiveness first so that we can get our sins out of the way and present the real petitions; we realize that forgiveness and right relationship with God *is* the gift and the source of the happiness we seek.

PRAYER. *Father, forgive our sins and heal our troubled minds.*

W HEN we share in God's saving love, we understand that *every need* can become the object of petition. Christ, who assumed all things in order to redeem all things, is glorified by what we ask the Father in his name.††

—No. 2633

NOV. 27

REFLECTION. In a loving family children bring everything to their parents and the parents are interested, whatever the topic. As our loving parent, there is nothing about our lives that God does not find intensely interesting, nothing that he does not long for us to share with him.

PRAYER. *Jesus, be Lord of all my life.*

† Lk 18:13.
†† Cf. Jn 14:13.

INCE Abraham, intercession—asking on behalf of another—has been characteristic of a heart attuned to God's mercy. In the age of the Church, Christian intercession participates in Christ's, as an expression of the communion of saints.

—No. 2635

NOV. 28

REFLECTION. All Christians who are "in Christ," in heaven and on earth, participate in the intercession of Christ before the Father. For Christians, praying for each other is part of our nature.

PRAYER. *Father, bless those who have asked for our prayers.*

S IN the prayer of petition, every event and need can become an offering of thanksgiving. —No. 2638

NOV. 29

REFLECTION. Christians who are tuned into what God is like are perpetually grateful. To thank God for everything that comes our way—good or bad—is to express the highest degree of faith in God's love for us. That kind of gratitude comes from a humble heart which knows that he really does have the whole world in his hands.

PRAYER. *We thank you, Lord, and we praise you, for all you have given us.*

RAISE is the form of prayer which recognizes most immediately that God is God. It lauds God for his own sake and gives him glory, quite beyond what he does, but simply because HE IS. —No. 2639

NOV. 30

REFLECTION. Praise is probably the least practiced type of prayer by Christians, and yet, it is our eternal destiny to praise God without ceasing. This fact underscores the truth that now we know God only in part, but when we see him face to face, pure praise will be our natural reaction and our greatest joy.

PRAYER. *Father, we praise you and we bless you.*

RAYER, formed by the liturgical life, draws everything into the love by which we are loved in Christ and which enables us to respond to him by loving as he has loved us. Love is the source of prayer; whoever draws from it reaches the summit of prayer. —No. 2658

DEC. 1

REFLECTION. Time and time again the *Catechism* brings everything back to love, the greatest of all virtues. It is the degree to which we love that reveals our own godliness.

PRAYER. *Father of love, you are love. Teach us the most excellent way.*

THERE is no other way of Christian prayer than Christ. Whether our prayer is communal or personal, vocal or interior, it has access to the Father only if we pray "in the name" of Jesus. The sacred humanity of Jesus is therefore the way by which the Holy Spirit teaches us to pray to God our Father.

—No. 2664

DEC.
2

REFLECTION. The Christian cannot understand any aspect of life apart from Christ. This is especially true in prayer, which must be done "in Christ" using his name.

PRAYER. *Jesus, may we use your name worthily that our prayers may be efficacious.*

THE one name that contains everything is the one that the Son of God received in his incarnation: JESUS. . . . The name "Jesus" contains all: God and man and the whole economy of creation and salvation. To pray "Jesus" is to invoke him and to call him within us.

—No. 2666

DEC.
3

REFLECTION. Once we understand the significance that is in a name, we begin to appreciate the power of the word "Jesus." Unfortunately, the power of that name is most often used to curse; imagine how powerful it is when used correctly—to bless.

PRAYER. *Jesus, give us a deep respect for your name.*

THE prayer of the Church venerates and honors the *Heart of Jesus* just as it invokes his most holy name. It adores the incarnate Word and his Heart which, out of love for men, he allowed to be pierced by our sins. —No. 2669

DEC. 4

REFLECTION. If the heart is the very core and center of the human being, then the Heart of Jesus contains the richest share of his divinity and therefore should occupy a special place in our life of prayer, contemplation, and mediation.

PRAYER. *Sacred Heart of Jesus, make our hearts like your own.*

EVERY time we begin to pray to Jesus it is the Holy Spirit who draws us on the way of prayer by his prevenient grace. . . . That is why the Church invites us to call upon the Holy Spirit every day, especially at the beginning and the end of every important action. —No. 2670

DEC. 5

REFLECTION. When we understand and appreciate the different movements of each person of the Trinity, we begin to know the ways of God and can more easily enter into the divine mystery of our lives.

PRAYER. *Come, Holy Spirit, with thy grace and heavenly aid.*

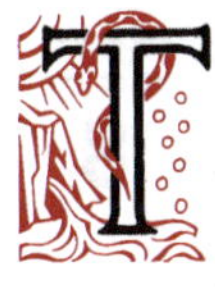

THE Holy Spirit, whose anointing permeates our whole being, is the interior Master of Christian prayer. He is the artisan of the living tradition of prayer. To be sure, there are as many paths of prayer as there are persons who pray, but it is the same Spirit acting in all and with all. —No. 2672

DEC. 6

REFLECTION. Among the three persons of the Trinity, the Holy Spirit inspires and facilitates our prayers. He is the active ingredient whose presence during prayer authenticates all our communication with the Father through the Son.

PRAYER. *Come, Holy Spirit, inspire us to pray in truth.*

BEGINNING with Mary's unique cooperation with the working of the Holy Spirit, the Churches developed their prayer to the holy Mother of God, centering it on the person of Christ manifested in his mysteries. —No. 2675

DEC. 7

REFLECTION. All Marian prayers, the Hail Mary, the Rosary, the Angelus, etc., find their center of gravity in Jesus and the mystery of his life. The placement of his sacred name and the meditation on his life provoked by Marian prayers gives them a Christocentric focus which Mary herself desires.

PRAYER. *Mary, reveal to us the blessed fruit of your womb, Jesus.*

ECAUSE she gives us Jesus, her son, Mary is Mother of God and our mother; we can entrust all our cares and petitions to her: she prays for us as she prayed for herself: "Let it be to me according to your word."† By entrusting ourselves to her prayer, we abandon ourselves to the will of God together with her: "Thy will be done." —No. 2677

DEC. 8

REFLECTION. When we feel the need for another's prayers we turn to someone close to God who models the true Christian life. No one fits this description better than Mary.

PRAYER. *Holy Mary, Mother of God, pray for us.*

RAYER is the life of the new heart. It ought to animate us at every moment. But we tend to forget him who is our life and our all. This is why the Fathers of the spiritual life . . . insist that prayer is a remembrance of God often awakened by the memory of the heart: "We must remember God more often than we draw breath."†† —No. 2697

DEC. 9

REFLECTION. Communion with God, which happens primarily through prayer, is the oxygen of our spiritual lives. This is why we must pray always.

PRAYER. *Jesus, be my life and my all.*

† Lk 1:38.

†† St. Gregory of Nazianzus, *Orat. theo.*, 27, 1, 4: PG 36, 16.

UT we cannot pray "at all times" if we do not pray at specific times, consciously willing it. These are the special times of Christian prayer, both in intensity and duration. —No. 2697

DEC. 10

REFLECTION. Efficacious spontaneous prayer springs from a life of structured prayer in ancient devotional and liturgical rhythms. The Church has preserved many for us: morning, evening, and meal prayers, the cycle of the liturgical year, and especially the Liturgy of the Word and the Eucharist.

PRAYER. *Lord, help us to learn the art of prayer from Holy Mother Church.*

HE need to involve the senses in interior prayer corresponds to a requirement of our human nature. We are body and spirit, and we experience the need to translate our feelings externally. We must pray with our whole being to give all power possible to our supplication. —No. 2702

DEC. 11

REFLECTION. Posture, environment, visual cues and other sensory stimuli are important factors in prayer which help (or hinder) the engagement of the whole person in communion with the God of spirit and matter.

PRAYER. *Jesus, teach us to give you our whole selves.*

EDITATION engages thought, imagination, emotion, and desire. This mobilization of faculties is necessary in order to deepen our convictions of faith, prompt the conversion of our heart, and strengthen our will to follow Christ. Christian prayer tries above all to meditate on the mysteries of Christ, as in *lectio divina* or the rosary. —No. 2708

DEC. 12

REFLECTION. Any rich relationship contains many ways of being together and different methods of communication. Our prayer life and our relationship with God are enriched by times of quiet meditation in the presence of the divine.

PRAYER. *Father, help us to meditate on you.*

ONTEMPLATION is a *gaze* of faith, fixed on Jesus. . . . This focus on Jesus is a renunciation of self. His gaze purifies our heart; the light of the countenance of Jesus illumines the eyes of our heart. . . . —No. 2715

DEC. 13

REFLECTION. At a certain point our prayer must go beyond word *and* thought to the simple realization of being in God's presence and the knowledge that he sees us, and that we are truly present to him.

PRAYER. *Father, the contemplation of your being gives us joy.*

RAYER is both a gift of grace and a determined response on our part. It always presupposes effort. The great figures of prayer . . . all teach us this: prayer is a battle. Against whom? Against ourselves and against the wiles of the tempter who does all he can to turn man away from prayer, away from union with God.

—No. 2725

DEC. 14

REFLECTION. Anything of value must be protected. So it is with the divine life. We must fight for it with vigilance against enemies without and enemies within.

PRAYER. *Jesus, strengthen our spiritual will.*

E PRAY as we live, because we live as we pray. If we do not want to act habitually according to the Spirit of Christ, neither can we pray habitually in his name.

—No. 2725

DEC. 15

REFLECTION. Some would say that anything can be a prayer. It is true that a walk in the woods, for example, *can* be a prayer, but surely not everyone who walks in the woods is praying. Prayer is always a conscious act that is shaped by the totality of our lives.

PRAYER. *Spirit of God, animate our hearts at all times.*

THE habitual difficulty in prayer is *distraction.* . . . To set about hunting down distractions would be to fall into their trap, when all that is necessary is to turn back to our heart: for a distraction reveals to us what we are attached to.

—No. 2729

DEC. 16

REFLECTION. The thoughts that come to distract our prayers can tell us much about ourselves and reveal where our heart lies. We can sanctify these thoughts when we offer them up to the Father along with our prayers.

PRAYER. *Holy Spirit, inspire single-minded focus in our prayers.*

THE most common yet most hidden temptation is our *lack of faith.* . . . Sometimes we turn to the Lord as a last resort, but do we really believe he is? Sometimes we enlist the Lord as an ally, but our heart remains presumptuous.

—No. 2732

DEC. 17

REFLECTION. In times of trouble we turn to God instinctively, but in good times he often ceases to exist. Such a "jack in the box" God is common, but true faith does not waver on God, but clings to him in love in any circumstance.

PRAYER. *Lord, be with us in prosperity and adversity.*

THE Gospel is this "Good News." Its first proclamation is summarized by St. Matthew in the Sermon on the Mount;† the prayer to our Father is at the center of this proclamation.

—No. 2763

DEC. 18

REFLECTION. The Our Father is the primary prayer of the Christian life; it is the perfect summation of all Christian prayers and the key to understanding communication with God. To pray the Our Father is to set our life in the context of the whole message of Christ.

PRAYER. *Lord, teach us to pray the Our Father.*

WHEN we pray to the Father, we are *in communion with him* and with his Son, Jesus Christ.†† Then we know and recognize him with an ever new sense of wonder. . . . For it is the glory of God that we should recognize him as "Father," the true God.

—No. 2781

DEC. 19

REFLECTION. We begin this most important of all prayers by standing shoulder to shoulder with Christ our brother as we call God, our Father. This unity with Christ and filial attachment to the Father is what makes this prayer so important.

PRAYER. *God, you are our Father.*

† Cf. Mt 5—7.

†† Cf. 1 Jn 1:3.

THE symbol of the heavens refers us back to the mystery of the covenant we are living when we pray to our Father. He is in heaven, his dwelling place; the Father's house is our homeland.

—No. 2795

DEC. 20

REFLECTION. If our true father is in heaven, then heaven is our homeland, where we belong, and the place where our heart and treasure lie. It is a powerful act of faith and hope to proclaim this.

PRAYER. *Our Father, who art in heaven.*

THE first series of petitions carries us toward him, for his own sake: *thy* name, *thy* kingdom, *thy* will! It is characteristic of love to think first of the one whom we love. In none of the three petitions do we mention ourselves; the burning desire, even anguish, of the beloved Son for his Father's glory seizes us.†

—No. 2804

DEC. 21

REFLECTION. As with the Creed and the Commandments, the Our Father begins with our creator. This is our starting point for all our prayers—God's presence, God's name, God's will.

PRAYER. *Hallowed be thy name; thy kingdom come; thy will be done.*

† Cf. Lk 22:44; 12:50.

THE second series of petitions unfolds . . . as an offering up of our expectations, that draws down upon itself the eyes of the Father of mercies. They go up from us and concern us from this very moment, in our present world: "give *us* . . . forgive *us* . . . lead *us* not . . . deliver *us*. . . . " —No. 2805

DEC. 22

REFLECTION. In the Our Father, Jesus teaches us our basic needs: sustenance for our bodies, forgiveness for our souls, protection for our spirits.

PRAYER. *Lord, watch over our souls, nourish our bodies, forgive our sins.*

ASKING the Father that his name be made holy draws us into his plan of loving kindness for the fullness of time, "according to his purpose which he set forth in Christ," that we might "be holy and blameless before him in love."† —No. 2807

DEC. 23

REFLECTION. God's name is always hallowed, but only when all men recognize and live this truth will all be right with the world. Our efforts to spread the good news are really nothing more than efforts to make holy his name among all people.

PRAYER. *Hallowed be thy name.*

† Eph 1:9, 4.

N THE Lord's Prayer, "thy kingdom come" refers primarily to the final coming of the reign of God through Christ's return.† But, far from distracting the Church from her mission in this present world, this desire commits her to it all the more strongly.

—No. 2818

DEC. 24

REFLECTION. In that grey area between God's control of the world right now and his ultimate complete reign in glory lies the world of human freedom—the source of much joy and suffering.

PRAYER. *Lord, may our actions bring peace and joy to the world.*

W

E ASK insistently for this loving plan to be fully realized on earth as it is already in heaven.

—No. 2823

DEC. 25

REFLECTION. When Christmas is celebrated joyfully and in a community of love and peace, on those perfect Christmas days when it seems the whole world is celebrating the birth of Christ, we catch a glimpse of the day when God's will will be done on earth, as it is in heaven.

PRAYER. *Father, grant that the peace and joy of this day will influence all the days of our life.*

† Cf. Titus 2:13.

Y PRAYER we can discern "what is the will of God" and obtain the endurance to do it.† Jesus teaches us that one enters the kingdom of heaven not by speaking words, but by doing "the will of my Father in heaven."†† —No. 2826

DEC. 26

REFLECTION. Everyone has dreamed of having a wish come true. There are so many things we pine for, yet no greater and more valuable wish could be granted to a human being than *to know and do the will of God.*

PRAYER. *Father, may your will be done by me today.*

"OUR daily bread" refers to the earthly nourishment necessary to everyone for subsistence, and also to the Bread of Life: the Word of God and the Body of Christ. It is received in God's "today," as the indispensable, (super-) essential nourishment of the feast of the coming Kingdom anticipated in the Eucharist. —No. 2861

DEC. 27

REFLECTION. There is a great economy in the phrase, "daily bread," designating at once all our basic bodily needs as well as our need for Christ's body and blood, the bread of life.

PRAYER. *Father, give us this day our daily bread.*

† Rom 12:2; cf. Eph 5:17; cf. Heb 10:36.
†† Mt 7:21.

THE fifth petition begs God's mercy for our offences, mercy which can penetrate our hearts only if we have learned to forgive our enemies, with the example and help of Christ. —No. 2862

DEC. 28

REFLECTION. The importance of forgiveness for the Christian is underscored by the fact that this is the only petition of the Our Father which has a condition attached to it!

PRAYER. *Father, forgive us our sins as we forgive those who have sinned against us.*

WHEN we say "lead us not into temptation" we are asking God not to allow us to take the path that leads to sin. This petition implores the Spirit of discernment and strength; it requests the grace of vigilance and final perseverance. —No. 2863

DEC. 29

REFLECTION. Temptation is one of the oddest experiences that human beings encounter. It is a unique combination of desire and pleasure, fear and danger. Only the wise and the strong can recognize it, battle and overcome it. It is better to avoid the things that cause us to be tempted.

PRAYER. *Father, lead us not into temptation.*

IN THE last petition, "but deliver us from evil," Christians pray to God with the Church to show forth the victory, already won by Christ, over the "ruler of this world," Satan, the angel personally opposed to God and to his plan of salvation.

—No. 2864

DEC. 30

REFLECTION. The presence of evil in a world made by a loving God is a great mystery. But we do know that it is not God's plan for us to feel the crushing blow of evil. Jesus urges us to pray that we might be spared from evil.

PRAYER. *Father, deliver us from all evil.*

BY THE final "Amen," we express our "fiat" concerning the seven petitions: "So be it."

—No. 2865

DEC. 31

REFLECTION. When we give our "Amen" to something, we are giving the strongest possible consent to the prayer or statement, as if to say, "I feel that this is true with my whole being and I consent." Jesus often used it at the beginning of his statements to underscore his deep conviction in what he was about to say. An "Amen" should not be taken, or given, lightly.

PRAYER. *Amen, Lord, I believe in you.*

PRAYER FOR ALL THINGS NECESSARY TO SALVATION

I BELIEVE, Lord, but may I believe more firmly.
I hope, but may I hope more securely.
I love, but may I love more ardently.
I grieve, but may I grieve more deeply.

I adore you as my first beginning.
I aspire after you as my last end.
I praise you as my perpetual benefactor.
I invoke you as my merciful protector.

Direct me by your wisdom.
Keep me in your grace.
Console me with your mercy.
Protect me with your power.

I offer you, O Lord,
my thoughts, that they may be about you;
my words, that they may be spoken for your glory;
my actions, that they may accord with your will;
my sufferings, that they may be accepted for your sake.

I desire whatever you desire.
I desire it because you desire it.
I desire it insofar as you desire it.
I desire it for as long as you desire it.

I pray, O Lord, that you will enlighten my mind,
inflame my will,
cleanse my heart,
and sanctify my soul.

May I repent of past sins,
repel future temptations,
correct wicked tendencies,
and cultivate virtuous ideals.

Good Lord, grant that I may love you,
renounce myself,

do good to my neighbor,
and be detached toward the world.

May I strive to obey my superiors,
support my inferiors,
aid my friends,
and spare my enemies.

Help me to overcome sensuality by self-denial,
avarice by liberality,
anger by meekness,
and tepidity by devotion.

Make me prudent in counsel,
steadfast in danger,
patient in adversity,
and humble in prosperity.

Grant, Lord, that I may be attentive at prayer,
temperate at meals,
diligent at work,
and constant in resolutions.

Let my conscience be upright,
my outward appearance be modest,
my conversation be edifying,
and my whole life be ordered.

Help me to labor to overcome nature,
to cooperate with your grace,
to keep your commandments,
and to further my salvation.

Teach me the futility of earthly things,
the greatness of Divine things,
the shortness of temporal things,
and the length of eternal things.

Grant that I may be prepared for death,
fear judgment,
avoid hell,
and obtain paradise—
through Christ our Lord.

Clement XI (1649-1721), *Pope and Scholar*

ABBREVIATIONS

Acts — Acts of the Apostles
AG — *Ad gentes*
Can. — Canon
Cann. — Canons
CCEO — *Corpus Canonum Ecclesiarum*
2 Chr — 2 Chronicles
CIC — *Codex Iuris Canonici*
Col — Colossians
1 Cor — 1 Corinthians
2 Cor — 2 Corinthians
CT — *Catechesi tradendae*
Deut — Deuteronomy
DS — Denzinger-Schönmetzer, *Enchiridion Symbolorum, definitionum et declarationum de rebus fidei et morum* (1965)
DV — *Dei Verbum*
En. in Ps — *Enarrationes in Psalmos*
Eph — Ephesians
Ex — Exodus
Expos. in symb. apost. — *Expositio in symbolum apostolicum*
Ezek — Ezekiel
FC — *Familiaris consortio*
Gal — Galatians
Gen — Genesis
GS — *Gaudium et spes*
Heb — Hebrews
Isa — Isaiah
Jas — James
Jn — John
1 Jn — 1 John
LG — *Lumen gentium*
Lk — Luke
Mk — Mark
MM — *Mater et magistra*
Mt — Matthew
NA — *Nostra aetate*
Neh — Nehemiah
Orat. theo. — *Orationes theologicae*
1 Pet — 1 Peter
2 Pet — 2 Peter
PG — J. P. Migne, ed., Patrologia Graeca (Paris, 1857-1866)
Phil — Philippians
PL — J. P. Migne, ed., Patrologia Latina (Paris, 1841-1855)
PO — *Presbyterorum ordinis*
Ps — Psalms
Rev — Revelation
Rom — Romans
SC — *Sacrosanctum concilium*
Sermo. — Sermon
Sir — Sirach
STh — *Summa theologiae*
Symbol. — Symbolorum
Titus — Titus
UR — *Unitatis redintegratio*
Wis — Wisdom

ISBN 978-1-937913-54-0
90000
9 781937 913540